Taormina, Sicily, Italy

Tourism

Author
Ibrahim Lloyd.

SONITTEC PUBLISHING. All rights reserved. No part of this publication may be reproduced, distributed, or transmitted in any form or by any means, including photocopying, recording, or other electronic or mechanical methods, without the prior written permission of the publisher, except in the case of brief quotations embodied in critical reviews and certain other noncommercial uses permitted by copyright law. For permission requests, write to the publisher, addressed "Attention: Permissions Coordinator," at the address below.

Copyright © 2019 Sonittec Publishing
All Rights Reserved

First Printed: 2019.

Publisher:
SONITTEC LTD
College House, 2nd
Floor
17 King Edwards
Road,
Ruislip
London
HA4 7AE

Table of Content

SUMMARY 1
INTRODUCTION 12
DISCOVER TAORMINA TOURISTIC HISTORY AND VALUE 17
TOURISM 24
   TAORMINA TOURIST INFORMATION 39
   THINGS TO DO IN TAORMINA: TOURIST ATTRACTIONS AND SIGHTS 50
      Giardini Naxos 65
      Castelmola, a Taormina excursion 75
      Porta Messina and Porta Catania 85
      The fountain in Piazza Duomo 86
      The Byzantine Madonna 88
      The San Domenico 89
      The Clock Tower 90
      The Gymnasium (The Naumachie) 91
      The Public Gardens 93
      The Arabian Necropolis 94
      Greek Theater of Taormina 95
      Parco Fluviale dell'Alcantra 96
      Isola Bella 97
         Aviary on Isola Bella 99
      Wunderbar 100
      Monuments 101
         The Greek-Roman Theatre 101
         Badia Vecchia 105
         Palazzo Corvaja 107
         The Antiquarium 110
         The Odeon 113
         Palazzo Duca di S. Stefano 115
         Palazzo Ciampoli 119
         Piazza Ix Aprile In Taormina 121
         Saracen Castle In Taormina 122
         Fountain Piazza Duomo In Taormina 123
      Churches 124

- Foods and Wine 130
- Surrunding Areas 135
- TOP THINGS TO DO IN TAORMINA 150
- WHERE TO STAY IN TAORMINA 162
  - The best places to stay in Taormina by selection 169
    - Hotels 169
      - Belmond Grand Hotel Timeo 169
      - Hotel Taodomus 171
      - Hotel Victoria 173
      - Casa Cuseni Maison De Charme 174
      - TaoApartments - Casa Vittoria 176
      - Villa Astoria 178
      - Hotel Villa Belvedere 179
      - Hotel Villa Ducale 180
      - Casa Lucia 182
      - UNAHOTELS Capotaormina 183
      - Panoramic Hotel 185
      - Villa Arianna B&B 186
- GETTING THERE 187
- EVENTS 189

Taormina, Sicily, Italy

Summary

Wonderful Benefits of Traveling

If there was one piece of advice I have for people today to experience more joy in life, it is to travel more. I don't mean taking vacations or going on pre-planning trips, I mean making the journey out to somewhere you've never gone before with an open schedule, to let life show you what opportunities were waiting for you that you couldn't have even imaged before.

Traveling is wonderful in many ways. It captures us with a sense of wanderlust and has us longing for more destinations to visit, cultures to experience, food to eat, and people to meet. As amazing as traveling is, most of us think we need to wait until our later years to really explore a lot of the world. I want to inspire you to travel more now and I will do that by sharing 9 wonderful benefits of traveling so you can take the leap of faith you've been waiting for.

You'll find a new purpose
To travel is to take a journey into yourself.
Traveling is an amazingly underrated investment in yourself. As you travel you're exposed to more new people, cultures, and lifestyles than you are living in your homeland all the time. With all the newness in your life, you're also opened to new insights, ways of seeing the world and living, which often gives people a new purpose for their lives. If you're feeling stuck on what your purpose is, what you want to do with your life, the career or educational path you want to pursue, go travel…you might just be surprised about what you

discover as a new sense of life purpose and direction.

You'll appreciate your home more

All travel has it's advantages. If the passenger visits better countries, he may learn to improve his own. And if fortune carries him to worse, he may learn to enjoy it.

When we spend time away from home, especially in a place where we don't have the same luxuries readily available to us...like a village in Fiji that runs without electricity...we become more aware and appreciative for the luxuries we have back at home. I remember a time where I visited my cousin in Argentina after she'd been living there for about a year. I was visiting her around Christmas time and brought her the new Harry Potter book along with some basic goods that you can find almost anywhere in Los Angeles. She was over joyous and filled with gratitude, like she just got the greatest gift in the world. In other parts of the world, like India and Ethiopia, people don't have as much access to clean drinking water...especially from what's readily available on tap. Traveling through areas like that really make us appreciate what we do have, and often can spark the movement of something to support people living there experience a greater quality of life.

You'll realize that your home is more than just where you grew up
No one realizes how beautiful it is to travel until he comes home and rests his head on his old, familiar pillow.
The more we travel, the more we realize that our home is so much more than the town, city, state and even country that we've grown up in; we realize that our home is the world, this planet, and

we become more conscious of how we can harmoniously live and support one another. And in that knowingness and state of consciousness, people like those supporting the movement of charity:water come into fruition.

You'll realize how little you actually knew about the world

The world is a book, and those who do not travel read only one page

There's concept, and then there's experience. When we travel, we may notice that some of the things we've heard about the world end up being very different than what we were indoctrinated and conditioned to believe. Many of the initial myths that get dispelled are often about traveling itself. Where you once may have thought it was too expensive and dangerous, you may realize how you can actually save more on your lifestyle expenses traveling the world than you do living at home. You may also realize how kind and friendly strangers can be, and how they are even willing to take care of you with a place to sleep at night. Beyond that, you have the whole world to learn about with every place you discover, every person you meet and every culture you experience.

You'll realize that we all share similar needs
Travel is fatal to prejudice, bigotry, and narrow-mindedness.
Tony Robbins has said many times that no matter what your background is, all human beings share 6 common needs. As you travel more, you notice the truth of this even more...and as that happens, you are more adept in being able to relate to people regardless of their background.

You'll realize that it's extremely easy to make friends

A journey is best measured in friends, rather than miles.

One of the first things I learned from traveling solo is how easy it is to make friends. Something magical happens in how people can show up more raw and real when they're out of their conditioned environment and open to express themselves without feeling judged. That rawness and realness ends up inspiring others to be authentic, and that's how you can become best friends with people when you've only known them for a few hours.

You'll experience the interconnectedness of humanity

Perhaps travel cannot prevent bigotry, but by demonstrating all peoples cry, laugh, eat, worry, and die, it can introduce the idea that if we try and understand each other, we may even become friends.

Just as we notice how we share similar needs, how our perspective of our home expands, and how we become close friends with others from different backgrounds and cultures, we begin to realize how we are all connected. This state of awareness is a jump in consciousness, and what I mean by that is in the way we perceive the world, the life experience and ourselves. Ken Wilber speaks about consciousness as spiral dynamics, each level of consciousness inclusive of the one previous. I feel that traveling often helps people experience a world-centric view of consciousness, and some even on that's integrated…able to see, understand and accept all states of consciousness, and utilizing the gifts of whatever is best and most appropriate in the moment.

You'll experience serendipity and synchronicity
Traveling is one of the easiest ways to become aware of the magic that weaves all of creation

together through serendipity and synchronicity with perfect timing.

Serendipity: luck that takes the form of finding valuable or pleasant things that are not looked for. And here's Synchronicity: coincidence of events that appear meaningfully related but do not seem to be causally connected

I'm going to share one story of how I experienced serendipity and synchronicity in Spain. It was early in the morning and it was time for me to return the motorcycle my friend had rented with me yesterday. She left very early in the morning on a flight home so it was my responsibility to return it. I woke up to a beautiful sunny morning in Spain and went out to the street to start the motorcycle. I started to drive, forgetting that the chain was left on the wheel. Having no previous experience with motorcycles, I realized I was in a predicament. Two minutes later, a car drove and parked behind me. I had a feeling that someone in that vehicle knew how to fix motorcycles and was going to help me remove the chain so I could return the motorcycle. As they got out, I spoke to them in Spanish, telling them what happened. One of them motioned the other to go on. He mentioned they were mechanics and here for a job, and that he could help me get the chain off…and he did. I thanked him and he seemed gratified to help a fellow soul on their way. In that moment, I realized that no matter what…the world is here to support me, which leads us to the last benefit of traveling.

You'll realize life is a wonderful gift

Life is either a daring adventure or nothing.

"Twenty years from now you will be more disappointed by the things that you didn't do than by the ones you did do. So throw off the bowlines.

Sail away from the safe harbor. Catch the trade winds in your sails. Explore. Dream. Discover."
Mark Twain

Life is a wonderful gift. It really is, and as we travel and experience more of the world and life, we often become overwhelmed with gratitude and appreciation for all the beautiful moments we enjoyed and people we've shared them with. More often than not, this is a realization that we can experience and take action from now while we're still alive with energy rather than stacking up regrets by the time we're on our death bed. Rather than waiting until you're saying "I wish I had", live so you can say "I'm glad I did".

Ibrahim Lloyd

Introduction

As soon as you arrive in Taormina, you will feel the magical, mythical atmosphere spread all around which has enchanted visitors from all over the world for years and years. Settled on a hill of the Monte Tauro, Taormina dominates two grand, sweeping bays below and on the southern side, the top of Mount Etna, the European highest active volcano, often capped with snow, offering to the visitors a breathtaking, dramatic and memorable view over almost one hundred miles of Mediterranean sea.

Taormina really seems to be born as a tourist resort since past times, when ancient people like the Sicels, Greeks, Romans, Byzantines, Saracens, Arabs, Normans and Spaniards chose it as their residential site thank to its favourable position, mild climate and magic atmosphere. Nowadays visitors can still find fine examples of Taormina's golden times: the splendid Greek Theatre, the Roman "Naumachiae", the 10th century Palazzo Corvaja, the 13th century Cathedral of Saint Nicolò, the 16th century Palace of the Dukes of Saint Stefano, the public gardens, the "Badia Vecchia" (Ancient Abbey) and many others.

The resort was first publicised by a trio of German artists. In 1787 J.W. Goethe discovered the beauties of Sicily and, in particular, of Taormina. He wrote the world known novel "Italian Journey", in which he describes the beauties of this land and its people and pronounced Taormina a "patch of paradise". The German painter Otto Geleng rose intereset in Parisan art galleries exibiting his paintings about this magical landscapes. His contemporary, the young prussian photographer Wilhelm von Gloeden settled down in 1880 and made Taormina famous to all conservative European cultural clubs with his artistic portraits of nude sheperd boys with the volcano Etna on the backstage.

Since then many important celebrities visited Taormina, electing it as their "escapade place" from chaotic city life. Patrik Brydone D.H. Lawrence, Truman Capote, Alexander Dumas, Anatole France, Andrè Gide, Paul Klee, Guy de Maupassant, Luigi Pirandello, John Steinbeck, Gustav Klimt, Elio Vittorini, Oscar Wilde, Richard Wagner, Johannes Brahms spent happy moments here. In more recent times movie, theatre and music celebrities such as Ingmar Bergmann, Francis Ford Coppola, Leonard Bergman, Marlene Dietrich, Greta Garbo, Federico Fellini, Cary Grant,

Tyrone Power, Gregory Peck, Marcello Mastroianni, Elisabeth Taylor, Woody Allen have spent pleasant and memorable holidays in the *Mediterranean pearl*.

Since the opening of the first hotel in 1874, Taormina has become one of the world top tourist destinations where visitors can experience a perfect combination of old times charming atmosphere, preservation of history and culture, an elegant and lively way of life to be enjoyed in relaxing walks through the old town pedestrian areas. The tourist has a lot to do and see: top level art performances at the Greek theatre, several painting exhibitions held in local palazzi and churces, fine elegant shopping along the famous "Corso Umberto" with its classical music cafès and pastry shops. Or visiting local art museums, taking naturalistic walks in the surrounding countryside, golfing at the nearby 18-holes green, enjoying the fantastic beaches at easy reach, where the mild Mediterranean climate allows to practise all water sports as swimming, scuba diving, sailing, windsurfing, or just sunbathing for nearly eight months a year and even more. Welcome to Taormina, the ultimate holiday paradise!

For those looking for the world known Sicilian cuisine, the town offers a wide choice of restaurants, trattorias and pizzerias, pastry-shops, bars, cafes, pubs and for any taste and budget. You won't find many fast food: Sicilians aren't really crazy about them! Come and see why… go to history.

Discover Taormina Touristic History and Value

Taormina the most beautiful town in Sicily, an old hilltop town full of history and culture and by the sea. Taormina is famous for its beauty, its incredible heritage in history, archaeology and architecture, as well as for its reputation in welcoming travellers. Taormina is perfectly situated to offer students easy access to the beautiful and historically important treasures of Sicily.

The village of Taormina is perched on a cliff overlooking the Ionian sea. Besides the ancient

Greek theatre, it has many old churches, lively bars, fine restaurants, and antique shops. Taormina is approximately a forty-five minute drive away from Europe's largest active volcano, Mount Etna.

Just south of Taormina is the Isola Bella, a nature reserve; and further south, situated beside a bay, is the popular seaside resort of Giardini Naxos. Isola Bella, the Bay of Mazzarrò, the Bay of Giardini Naxos, the Beach of Spisone, those are among the most famous beaches in Italy. Tours of the Capo Sant' Andrea grottos are also available.

For walkers, the surroundings of Taormina are also a beautiful paradise. There are several trails leading down to the sea and up to the picturesque village of Castelmola, and to the top of the highest mountain in the area, Monte Venere, where one of the three Greek temples of Venus is rumoured to have existed.

Taormina's first important tourist was Johann Wolfgang Goethe who dedicated exalting pages to the city in his book entitled Italian Journey, but perhaps it was the German painter Otto Geleng's views that made its beauty talked about throughout Europe and turned the site into a famous tourist center. The artist arrived in Sicily at the age of 20 in search of new subjects for his paintings. On his way through Taormina he was so enamoured by the landscape that he decided to stop for part of the winter. Geleng began to paint everything that Taormina offered: ruins, sea, mountains, none of which were familiar to the rest of Europe. When his paintings were later exhibited in Berlin and Paris, many critics accused Geleng of having an 'unbridled imagination'. At that, Geleng challenged them all to go to Taormina with him, promising that he would pay everyone's expenses if he were not telling the truth.

During the early 20th century the town became a colony of expatriate artists, writers, and intellectuals. D. H. Lawrence stayed here at the "Fontana Vecchia" from 1920 to 1922, and wrote a number of his poems, novels (probably including also Lady Chatterley's Lover), short stories, and essays, and a travel book. Thirty years later, from April 1950 through September 1951, the same villa was home to Truman Capote, who wrote of his stay in the essay "Fontana Vecchia." Charles Webster Leadbeater, the theosophical author, found out that Taormina had the right magnetics fields for Jiddu Krishnamurti to develop his talents, so the young Krishnamurti dwelt here from time to time. Halldór Laxness, the Icelandic author who won the Nobel prize for literature in 1955, worked here on the first modern Icelandic novel, Vefarinn mikli frá Kasmír. Between 1948 and 1999 the English writer Daphne Phelps lived in the Casa Cuseni designed and built by Robert Hawthorn Kitson in 1905, and entertained various friends including Bertrand Russell, Roald Dahl, and Tennessee Williams.

Many manifestations and events are organized during the summer in Taormina. The exceptional stage for pop and classical concerts, opera and important performances often recorded by television is the ancient Greek Theatre. Since 1983, the mostkkk important performances are realized by Taormina Arte, the cultural institution which organizes one of the most famous music, theatre and dance festivals. Within the program of Taormina Arte there is the Taormina Film Fest, the well-known cinema festival, dating from 1960.

Access to the beaches is very easy. From the center of Taormina, in 2 minutes, a cable-car connects Taormina to the beaches. Isola Bella, the Bay of Mazzarrò, the Bay of Giardini Naxos, the Beach of Spisone, those are among the most famous beaches in Italy.

Taormina plays a fundamental role as one of the most important archaeological locations in Italy. In fact, the Greeks, fathers of Italian and European culture, settled their first colony in Italy exactly here in the Bay of Naxos, in 735 BC.. Taormina is home to one of the most famous Greek Theatres in the world. Here, in summertime the main events of the International Film, Music, Dance and Theatre Festival of Taormina Arte take place.

Along with the different dominations that conquered Sicily, many important monuments and buildings were built in Taormina by the Greeks, the

Romans, the Byzantines, the Arabs, the Swebians, the Normans, the Spanish, the French, and the entire XIX European aristocracy have all left their "footprints", in Taormina in the form of beautiful buildings, monuments, churches, villas, parks and castles.

Watch our video or take a virtual tour of Taormina or have a look at our photo album, and learn more about the history, the monuments and the views of our town.

Taormina offers many opportunities in the way of hotels, restaurants, bars, discos, entertainment and sports.

With the aim of offering to you a wider cultural experience during your stay in Taormina and in Sicily, our Centre for Italian Studies offers a variety of "Italian plus…" programs, including:

Tourism

Taormina is a fascinating ancient town located in the Province of Messina, known worldwide for its impressive history, wonderful monuments and breathtaking landscape.

(Taormina) is one of the most interesting tourist destinations in Sicily, it is known worldwide for its landscape, natural beauties, seashore and its wonderful monuments. This charming city is located 200 meters above the sea level on a piece of land shaped like a natural terrace, from which it is possible to enjoy an amazing view of the surrounding area framed by the majestic (Mount Etna). Tourism is part of the city's life all year long, encouraged not only by its natural and cultural beauties, but also by very well working accommodation and recreational facilities, in addition to the typical Sicilian warmth.

Taormina has always been a renowned tourist destination, and through the centuries it hosted important writers like Goethe, Maupassant, D. H. Lawrence, A. France, Oscar Wilde, Brahms, and important personalities such as William II of Germany, the noblewoman Florence Trevelyan, the stylist Christian Dior, the German painter Geleng. It has also been a movie set chosen by many directors like Michelangelo Antonioni, who chose Taormina as the location for one of his best film "L'avventura"(1960).

Thanks to its wide variety of attractions, Taormina offers a series of different itineraries where visitors can discover its incredible monuments such as the

Cathedral of San Nicolò, the famous Theatre, the aristocratic buildings and the wonderful natural environments characterised by its public gardens, the beautiful beaches and the Alcantara gorges.

Taormina is rich in history and cultural attractions, the most important (monuments) of the city are:

the (Odeon is a small Roman theatre, built on the ruins of an ancient Greek temple in the II century BC, during the empire of Caesar Augustus Octavian. It hosted some of the most important musical and literary events of the ancient city dedicated only to the aristocratic part of the society. This charming theatre was made of clay bricks and its architecture reproduces the structure of Taormina's bigger (Greek-Roman theatre). It is divided in three main areas: the scaenae frons (the scene), the orchestra and the cavea (the seating section). The scene was characterised by a temple dedicated to Aphrodite, the goddess of love and beauty. The cavea was divided in five different sections, and it could contain about 200 people.

the (Public Garden Villa Comunale) was built by Florence Trevelyan, a British noblewoman who moved to Taormina after her mother's death. This little park is a good spot where get a relaxing rest and repair from the heat during the hottest summer days. This beautiful garden offers an enchanting view of the coast, the Naxos Gardens, and Mount Etna. Lady Florence Trevelyan created the park with a typical English style, filling the green area with a great variety of plants and flowers coming from all over the world and with many small buildings used as bird-watching spots. The most characteristic building located in the garden is "The Beehive", a small construction which reminds the shape of a beehive.

the (Alcantara Gorges) also known as *Larderia Gorges* or *Francavilla Gorges* are located in the Alcantara Valley, in Sicily. These gorges can reach a height of 25 meters, creating an impressive natural canyon. This particular kind of landscape hasn't been created by the slow work of water during the century. It has been created by the violent earthquakes that hit the area over time. The earthquakes broke the basaltic lakes that occupied the area letting the river's water insinuate inside the cracks.

The (Azzurra cave is located few meters away from the wonderful beach (Isola Bella). The cave offers a very evocative sight, thanks to the effect given by the light reflecting on the water and to it prominent marine flora. This area is a perfect location for (scuba diving and snorkeling) lovers: its underwater landscape is one of the most rich and fascinating of the whole coast.

The (Isola Bella) beach, also known as "the pearl of the Mediterranean", is a nature reserve. Named by the German Baron Wilhelm von Gloeden, who helped spreading worldwide the knowledge about the island's artistic value, this charming island was bought by Lady Florence Trevelyan in 1890 to grow the tropical plants that she wanted to put in her private garden (the Public Garden of Taormina). The Region established the nature reserve in 1998 to protect this incredible natural environment which is now managed by WWF.

(Palazzo Corvaja) houses the (Museum of Popular Arts and Traditions). This ancient building was created in the 11th century, during the Arab occupation of Sicily, and through time many changes have been made to its structure. The façade, made with the typical stone of Taormina, shows small mullioned windows with pointed arches and beautiful Corinthian capitals. It is also enriched by two bands of dark igneous stone.

The (Cathedral) is a medieval church dedicated to Saint Nicola di Bari. It was built in the 13th century on the ruins of an ancient church. The building was renovated in the 15th and 16th century. The Cathedral has a Latin cross plan, with three naves and three apses and the central nave is held up by six Taormina pink marble columns with flowers sculpted on their capitals. This columns might have been taken from the Greek-Roman theatre. Because of its austere medieval architecture and its external fortifications, the church is also called "the Fortress Cathedral". The cathedral has a great artistic value, especially the big central rose window showing a stunning Renaissance style. The church includes an impressive Byzantine Madonna which was found inside an old well, probably hidden there to save this beautiful work of art from the Arab invasion.

The (Palazzo Duca Santo Stefano), built in the 14th century, is a masterpiece of the Sicilian Gothic style, mixed with Arab and Norman traditional elements.

The façade shows a Norman framework, enriched by decorative elements coming from the Arab artistic tradition which were made using dark lava stone and the precious white stone from Siracusa. The palace is built on three levels. A pink granite column, taken from the Greek theatre, is located in the middle of the inner building. On the second floor there are four impressive windows characterised by a fascinating Gothic style. Today the building hosts the artistic foundation dedicated to the Sicilian artist Giuseppe Mazzullo and during the summer time its garden is a perfect location for many artistic and cultural events.

The (Church of San Giuseppe della Pia Società Salesiana), is located near the Clock Tower, also known as the "Torre di Mezzo". The church was built between the end of the 17th and the beginning of the 18th century with a typical Baroque style. The façade shows a big main entrance, made with Taormina marbles of different colours, and two small side entrances made with the white stone from Siracusa. The church has only one nave, and in the middle of the nave there is a small vault with a painting depicting Saint Giovanni Bosco as a child standing between Jesus and the Virgin Mary.

The (Church of San Pietro e Paolo) is the oldest Christian church in Taormina. It was built on the ruins of an ancient Greek temple located in the centre of the Arab necropolis. Its façade is dating back to the 18th century, is a simple doorway with the jambs and the architrave made with the typical stone from Taormina as well as the architrave with a full-centre arch made. The interior includes some interesting frescos and two majestic golden statues portraying Saint Peter and Saint Paul dating back to the 15th century.

The (Church Sanctuary of S.Maria della Rocca), built in the 12th century, was restored in 1600. It is erected on a small hill that dominates Taormina, from which it is possible to enjoy a breath-taking sight on Taormina's surroundings. Close to the church it is possible to visit an other wonderful holy place such as the(church of Saint Antonio) and (Convent of the Friars Minor Capuchin) which was built in 1559.

The (Saracen Castle) is located on Mount Tauro, 400 meters above the sea level. Thanks to its location, the castle could control the whole Alcantara River's valley. According to the tradition, the castle was built by Arabs. Under the Reign of Federico II, also known as "Stupor Mundi" thanks to his intellectual, political and military abilities, the castle was given to a Castilian nobleman. The outer walls have been kept very well, while almost all the inside walls collapsed.

The (Badia Vecchia) was built in the 14th century as a watchtower to protect the village from the barbarian invasions. This building is a beautiful example of the 13th century's Gothic architecture, even if it was modified several times in the later centuries. A decoration made with igneous and white stone inlays embellishes the palace's outer walls dividing the first from the second floor. The Badia Vecchia hosts the (Archeological Museum), which contains important findings from the Greek domination dating back to the 4th century BC, some ceramics and rare objects from the Roman period.

The (Clock Tower) or "Middle Door" built in the 12th century, was completely destroyed during the Luis XIV invasion in 1676. It was re-built in 1679 thanks to the will of the inhabitants of Taormina, who added the big clock on the top of the tower. Since then it has been called "the watch tower" instead of "the Middle Door".

Close to the theatre and the forum (today is piazza Vittorio Emanuele) rises the great wall of (Naumachia), another example of the Roman architecture. This ruins are part of the ancient Gymnasium, also known as Giardinazzo. It was the place where young men were educated and trained to take part to the Olympic Games. Philip of Orville improperly called this space "Naumachia" to describe this rectangular closed shape.

[Visitors have truly the possibility to enjoy their spare time in different activities. For those fond of sports the sweet climate allows to practice any kind of sport. By every beach even during winter time one can enjoy water sports such as wind-surfing, sailing, fishing, scuba-diving, canoeing, snorkeling or ... just jogging. In some beautiful nearby hilly villages there are international parafly clubs where one can also take lessons by professional teachers.

At approximately 4 Km from the Picciolo lies the Town of Linguaglossa, point of departure of most excursions heading into the Mt. Etna Nature Park. On the other side, at 8 Kms, one of most extraordinary monuments of nature: the

"Alcantara Gorges", a terrific natural phenomena with lava caves and falls, the "feather in the cap" of the Alcantara River Park, The One and Only River Park in Sicily. Crossing by foot a part of this river is a very unique experience even if you can do that only from May to September when the water level is low and when the hot temperature of the days help to deal with the freezing, really freezing!, waters.

If you are not a sports lover, you can find extremely appealing to shop in town. Along the famous car-free main walking street "Corso Umberto", visitors can enjoy the best Italian shopping stores at reasonable prices, certainly better than those in major Italian cities. Moreover the town offers a wide choice of selected unusual charming shops to purchase typical Sicilian products such as the renowned hand made ceramics or the elegant antiquities shops ,the delicatessen stores with plenty of local wines and other gourmet items or those selling fine leather, wrought iron and wooden products so known world-wide. For those looking for relaxation, you can find Health & Beauty programs in several hotels and Beauty farms straight in the town center as well as International hair stylist.

If you are a great reader, you can have free access to the public library in Piazza IX Aprile , one of the town 's main piazzas; here you can find free Italian and International newspapers and magazines, important English books about Sicily or Taormina and antique books just only to be admired! Finally if you really want to feel at ease like a true Sicilian, just buy your favorite paper, sit down at some of the several elegant open air cafès, forget what time it is, order your favorite drink or maybe a cappuccino, enjoy the piano playing, breath deeply the sweet atmosphere all around you and just relax ... that's probably the best treat of Taormina!!!]

Taormina tourist information

Sicily's most famous and long-established tourist resort, with a picturesque setting, wonderful views and ancient ruins

One of Italy's most historic holiday resorts, Taormina is a picturesque small town perched on a slope high above the Ionian Sea on the eastern coast of Sicily. A popular and fashionable destination for well over a century, Taormina's hotels and restaurants are very experienced at welcoming foreign tourists. Many of these are fairly expensive, including some fabulous luxury options. However, visitors don't have to spend a fortune to enjoy the town's principal attractions - the views, the scenery, the atmosphere.

Close to the site of one of the earliest colonies founded by the Ancient Greeks in Sicily, Taormina became a thriving Greek and then Roman town. The size and elegance of the town cathedral and many of its buildings are evidence of Taormina's moderate prosperity over the centuries. By the end of the 19th century this picturesque and ancient town was already on the tourist trail, with famous visitors including Oscar Wilde, Richard Wagner and Tsar Nicholas II. Over the last decades travellers have come for the views, the ancient ruins, the seaside, the town's film festival, an outdoor theatre season, the fine hotels and more. A classy honeymoon destination or a cheap and cheerful excursion from a cruise ship, Taormina has a lot to offer all kinds of visitor. As a consequence, of course, this small town is sometimes so crowded it can feel like a victim of its own success.

Accommodation is cheaper out of season, and the little town is less packed, too. March, April and May are good months to enjoy sunshine, the flowers and relatively-uncrowded streets and restaurants. Autumn in Sicily can feature heavy rainstorms, but also plenty of sunshine. On the negative side, out of season you may find hotel swimming pools emptied, building works underway around town, and little buzz in the nightlife.

Taormina is the one destination in Sicily, and probably the one Italian destination south of the Amalfi Coast, where tourism is really well-established and dominates the entire character of the town. So for less experienced travellers, non-Europeans, and newcomers to Italy, it is a manageable and reassuring place to stay. English is widely spoken, but the town still values its traditions and you'll enjoy Sicilian food and a fair amount of Italian atmosphere. If you are a seasoned Italy traveller and looking for authentic Sicily, Taormina is still worth visiting, though you'd probably prefer to combine it with other, less-touristy spots.

Where to stay in Taormina

Travel to Taormina

Taormina is straightforward to reach. The nearest airport is Catania Fontanarossa, with seasonal flights from the UK and other European countries, and there is a regular bus service from the airport to Taormina. The journey takes about an hour and a half, and there are services throughout the daytime and early evening. You should check timetables before travelling, via link on the right-hand links panel. Tickets can be booked online in advance or at kiosks outside the airport terminal building. If you are arriving late and relying on public transport, it may be best to stay overnight in Catania, or arrange a taxi transfer through your Taormina hotel.

The bus terminal in Taormina is on on Via Luigi Pirandello, a short walk downhill from the town centre, so you will still have to drag your suitcases to your accommodation (check the distance before committing to this), or arrange for a taxi.

Bus travel is often the quickest way between towns in Sicily, as the island's rail network is limited; timetables for most useful inter-city bus companies can be checked via the link on the right. Taormina does have a railway station, situated by the sea, far below the town. The station also serves the coastal settlement of Giardini Naxos, and the station is therefore named Taormina -

Giardini. The station is on the railway line that connects Messina, Catania and Siracusa, and is also served by long-distance trains from Rome.

Small local buses serve Taormina and its local districts, including the station. Tickets can be bought from the driver, or at the station newsagents (*edicola*). The zig-zagging journey up to Taormina takes about ten minutes. Longer distance buses, including the one from Catania airport, stop in Giardini Naxos as well as in Taormina.

A cable-car connects Taormina with the seaside at Mazzarò, for visits to the beach and Isola Bella. There are also sightseeing buses which run up to Castelmola and down to Giardini Naxos and Mazzarò; although more expensive than local buses, they are aimed at tourists and you can get reasonable value from a 24-hour ticket if you plan your time efficiently.

If you are planning to drive to Taormina, check the parking provision when you are choosing accommodation, and ask your hotel for directions; the central lanes are partly pedestrianised . There are large fee-charging car parks outside the town centre, including the Parking Garage Lumbi, with a bus connection to the centre.

Taormina tourist information

There is a tourist information office on the ground floor of Palazzo Corvaja, by Piazza Vittorio Emanuele. You may not find it particularly helpful or welcoming though - on my last visit staff were unhelpful and even hostile to visitors, perhaps worn down by the large crowds of daytripping tour groups stripping their offices of maps. It's worth trying to obtain a map or studying the information they have pinned to their walls, though. Doing some online research and printing out/downloading relevant timetables is good preparation for a trip. In my experience commercial businesses such as hotels and restaurants were much more helpful in every way.

On a budget

There are several fairly economical B&Bs in Taormina, but an alternative is to stay in one of the nearby seaside towns instead. You'll be closer to the beach, and can take a bus up to Taormina itself. Travelling out of season will also obtain you cheaper accommodation rates.

If you're on a tight budget, an economical option is to have at least one picnic meal or takeaway per day. Small general stores will make you up a roll from their products on display (cheese, ham etc) for a few euros, and the town has a choice of takeaways where you can buy pizza slices, arancini and other Sicilian street food for a cheap meal. You can fill up your water bottle at drinking fountains, and eat your picnics in the public gardens.

Taormina restaurants

Taormina has a good choice of restaurants, and some are quite reasonably-priced, although you should be prepared to pay a cover charge for each diner. Although the town's restaurants cater primarily for a foreign, tourist clientele, and do it well, you can still find traditional family-run restaurants with an authentic local ambience and decent prices. Some of these can be found at either end of the town, around and outside the old city gates. I've eaten at Trattoria da Ugo (Viale Arcageta 2), a nice rustic-feeling trattoria. For something a bit different, Babilonia (via Timoleone 10) has a romantic location in the leafy garden of a language school, and offers stylish versions of classic Sicilian dishes. With indoor and outdoor tables in the historic centre, Vecchia Taormina (Vico Ebrei 3) is an unpretentious osteria-pizzeria with a friendly atmosphere and a good range of pizzas.

Taormina itineraries: how to visit

Many visitors choose simply to spend their entire holiday in Taormina. This allows for a relaxing, stress-free break. It's possible to take excursions from Taormina to Catania, Savoca, Etna or further afield, by public transport or organised tours. A trip up to Castelmola and some time spent down by the sea at Giardini Naxos and Mazzarò is a pleasant way to pass time. Then of course there is the pottering through the pretty town, leisurely aperitivi and long, enjoyable meals.

Travellers planning a more active trip can combine Taormina with a longer tour around Sicily by hire-car or public transport, or a less ambitious exploration of this eastern end of the island. Siracusa and Catania are both attractive and interesting cities to stay in, and for a very varied trip you could follow Taormina with a trip to the beautiful and volcanic Aeolian islands. The main port for the islands is Milazzo, reachable by bus from Taormina with a change at Messina, or by taxi transfer. There are also occasional ferries from Messina in summer.

One excellent itinerary without too much travel is to spend a night or two in Catania seeing the sights, take a bus to Taormina, spend several days in Taormina, then head off the beaten track to the hill village of Savoca for a night or two, to experience a totally contrasting village atmosphere.

Things to do in Taormina: Tourist attractions and sights

Taormina has one truly unmissable tourist sight, its Greek Theatre, but the town, its location and its views are attractions in themselves. It's easy to spend a couple of days pottering around the town and its environs; longer if you plan to relax by the sea or a pool, or to roam further afield.

Explore the town

Taormina's great popularity over more than a century is largely about its atmosphere, views and charm. Although in size it would generally be considered a small town, the historic centre feels like a well-to-do hill village turned into a resort with a glossy sheen of glamour.

Exploring the historic centre can take as much as several hours, if you are looking around shops and studios, stopping at a cafe, buying an ice-cream and admiring views. The handsome principal thoroughfare, Corso Umberto, is mostly pedestrianised and ideal for strolling and window-shopping. Halfway along is the panoramic Piazza IX Aprile, a focal point for visitors, where you can sit on benches and admire the town's wonderful views over the sea and towards Etna. A drink at the outdoor tables of the historic Caffè Wunderbar is a pricey treat, but you'll be following in the footsteps of famous visitors including Tenessee Williams and Elizabeth Taylor.

Picturesque alleys and staircases above and below the Corso are interesting to explore, while if you want to stretch your legs further there are attractive walks up into the hills, or down to the sea. Given its compact size, Taormina has a huge range of bars, cafes and restaurants where you can while away pleasant hours while admiring the views. Shop sell everything from cheap souvenirs to high-end jewellery. You can find designer boutiques, including big names, as well as more 'local' businesses selling art works and pretty traditional ceramics. Dining options range from restaurants offering Sicilian, Italian and international cuisine, to street food outlets and *gelaterie* offering spectacular *gelato* flavours and ice slush *granite*.

Corso Umberto runs through the historic centre between the two historic town gateways, Porta Catania to the south-west and Porta Messina to the north-east. Close to the Porta Catania end of the street is Taormina's picturesque cathedral, (Cattedrale/Duomo), dedicated to St Nicholas. Attractive inside and out, the building was founded in the thirteenth century on the site of an earlier church, was rebuilt in the fiteenth-sixteenth centuries, and has features from several eras including columns of pink Taormina marble which originally came from the Greek Theatre. Outside the church, the dignified Piazza Duomo features one of the most recognisable symbols of the town, a seventeenth-century fountain bearing a very curious sculpture of a female version of a Minotaur. The fountain is known as the Quattro Fontane for its four subsidiary spouts.

Another, very different, church can be found by energetic visitors up the slopes above the town. A stepped footpath climbs up to the Santuario della Madonna della Rocca, a tiny church cut into the rocks. A little further up Monte Tauro, the mountain across whose slopes Taormina is spread, is a ruined fortress, the Castello Saraceno, theoretically open to the public, though closed for restoration at the time of writing. This outing uphill from the centre of Taormina is not particularly demanding, and it affords marvellous views in several directions.

Tour the Greek Theatre and other ruins

Taormina's greatest tourist attraction is the Teatro Greco, a Greco-Roman theatre built into a rocky hillside just a couple of minutes off Corso Umberto. Although generally known as the 'Greek' Theatre, Taormina's historic open-air theatre owes much of its present appearance to the Romans, the Greeks' successors in Sicily. Designed with an unsurpassable backdrop of blue sea, coastline, distant smoking Etna, and inland mountains, the theatre was founded by the Greeks in the third century BC.

In the first century AD, when Taormina was a significant Roman town, the Romans adapted the theatre to suit their more bloodthirsty tastes, stripping out seating to make more room for gladiatorial shows. Nowadays, dodging tour parties, you can wander around the theatre complex: the stage and backstage areas, as well as panoramic viewpoints up on the crags behind, each one breathtaking due to the theatre's position on a rocky spur of land extending towards the sea, far below. The curving rows of seats are a suntrap and a wonderful place to sit and dream away an hour or two. In the summer an arts festival (Taormina Arte) takes place here.

As well as the Greek Theatre, there are several other archaeological sites to be discovered around Taormina. Not far from the Teatro Greco, around the back of the Chiesa di Santa Caterina, are the ruins of a smaller Augustan-era theatre, which can be viewed through railings on the street (a small section of paving is also visible inside the church). Below Corso Umberto you'll find the 'Naumachie' (on Via Naumachie), a massive wall whose arched niches concealed a vast water cistern as well as buttressing the road above.

The strip of land in front of this wall has been made into a narrow public garden. A number of ancient necropoli are dotted around the area: some Byzantine grave-niches are visible on Via Pirandello just below the Belvedere, and a more dramatic necropolis above the town can be seen from the Castelmola - Taormina footpath. If you're interested in the ancient world and Sicily's Greek history, you should also fit in a visit to the display cabinets on Isola Bella, and the extensive ruins of Greek Naxos at Giardini Naxos, both described below.

Soak up the view

It would be hard to beat the views from Taormina on a clear day. Some of the best places for enjoying the vista are the panoramic terrace of Piazza IX Aprile on Corso Umberto, the Teatro Greco and the public gardens. A walk down Via

Pirandello or Via Guardiola Vecchia brings you to the Belvedere where the two roads meet. This look-out point offers seats to sit on and a great view along the coastline. For views over Taormina itself, head uphill to the Madonna della Rocca, or higher, to the village of Castelmola.

If you're prepared to splash out on a treat, the Grand Hotel Timeo (see Where to stay in Taormina) is a wonderful venue for an aperitivo, with bar tables on a terrace with views over the hotel's gardens and towards Etna which are particularly glorious at sunset. Be warned: this is a lavish but expensive experience.

Relax in the Trevelyan Gardens

Known by various names including the Villa Comunale, the Giardino Trevelyan and the Parco Duchi di Cesarò, the public park on Via Bagnoli Croce is a pretty and peaceful spot. An English-style garden, it was designed by Florence Trevelyan, who lived in Taormina at the end of the nineteenth century. A panoramic walkway lined with benches faces the view over the sea and Etna, while flower-beds, lawns, hedges, trees and bushes spread over the large terrace. There are several fascinating follies to admire, including cottages and towers, as well as a collection of caged birds, some old artillery, a children's play area and a bar (the latter two are not always open).

Visit a museum

Taormina has small but interesting collections of archaeological and folk artefacts which have been shifted around different exhibition venues in recent years - asking at the tourist office or your hotel should help you to locate current exhibitions. At the time of writing you can see a few showcases of archaeological finds at Isola Bella (see below), including a rather exciting sword, probably dating to the Byzantine era, which was found in the sea near the island. Other exhibits can be seen in the little Antiquarium within the Teatro Greco complex. Palazzo Corvaja, home of the tourist information office, also houses exhibitions.

Potentially even more interesting is the Museo Siciliano di Arti e Tradizioni Popolari, a collection relating to more recent 'folk' history of Taormina and the surrounding area. Housed at the time of writing in the ex Chiesa di San Francesco di Paolo, outside the Porta Catania up Viale Apollo Arcageta, this is a rather charming overview of 'people's history'. There are not-particularly-expert paintings of Sicilian families, wooden carvings of saints and odd bits of furniture.

Best of all are the ex-votos, small and often amateurish paintings produced as offerings, depicting mishaps and tragedies averted, with thanks to the saint who saved the day. Often touching, sometimes amusing, these include scenes of cat attacks, lava-flows from the erupting Etna, a tennis accident and a father shooting and injuring the son he mistook for an intruder. If you're interested in the history, traditions and everyday life of Sicily, it is really worth seeking out this under-visited attraction (ask locally about the current opening times, or any changes to location).

Paddle out to Isola Bella or relax on a beach

Taormina is situated high above the sea, with views over the beaches below, including the beautiful bay of Isola Bella. Isola Bella itself is a small and rocky islet which, like the public gardens, once belonged to Florence Trevelyan, who built a small house and planted a garden here. Nowadays it is a curious and atmospheric spot, with rocks, tropical vegetation, crumbling sculptural features and empty pools, grottoes and summer houses. Inside the uninhabited villa is a small exhibition of historic artefacts.

As well as being an unusual and eccentric garden/museum, it may be the only tourist attraction approached by splashing through waves, depending on sea conditions: attached by a narrow spit of sand and pebbles, visitors have to hoik up their clothing, take off their shoes and wade from the beach. There's a small admission charge, which is well worth paying for the experience.

For the energetic it's possible to descend to the sea on foot, either to the bay at Mazzarò or that of Isola Bella (from the Belvedere on Via Luigi

Pirandello). A cable-car (*funivia*) runs from Taormina down to Mazzarò, and both public and tour buses connect Taormina with the seashore.

Head up to Castelmola

Castelmola is a classic Sicilian hill village perched dramatically on a rocky hilltop above Taormina. It's a popular excursion from Taormina, reachable by bus or on foot. There are a few bars and trattorie for visitors, but it also retains an authentic and historic atmosphere.

Visit Giardini Naxos

Spread along wide bay below Taormina, south of the beaches described above, Giardini Naxos is a seaside resort in its own right. As well as a beach and boat trips, it also offers the chance to explore the ruins of the first ancient Greek colony in Sicily.

Take an excursion: volcano, Montalbano, ruins or cities

If you're staying more than two or three days in Taormina you may fancy an excursion of Sicily's attractions. A number of organised tourist excursions depart from the bus terminal, to destinations including Agrigento, Piazza Armerina, a 'Montalbano' tour and Savoca. These should be booked in advance, either online or in Taormina itself. If you're staying only in Taormina, and have no plans to return to Sicily, these coach trips offer a good chance to see some more of the island. But bear in mind that some of the destinations visited are a long drive away and the outings may be tiring as well as expensive.

The excursions mentioned above are definitely easier to make on an organised trip. But there are other destinations which are straightforward and much cheaper to visit by public transport, which will also give you more flexibility. Frequent buses run to the interesting city of Catania. By catching a local bus or taxi down to Taormina's railway station, you can easily and comfortably visit Catania or Messina or Siracusa, all on the same railway line.

One of the most interesting day trips from Taormina, and one for which Taormina is a very sensible base, is to Sicily's great, active volcano, (Mount) Etna. Local firms organise outings in coaches and jeeps, with a range of options, from adventurous ascents which approach the summit, to educational tours of the volcano's slopes, visiting the lava trails from past eruptions as well as sampling local food and drink. I took a small-group tour with Etna People, which was a fascinating and informative experience.

Giardini Naxos

Giardini Naxos is a seaside resort strung along a wide bay below the famous mountainside resort Taormina on the eastern coast of Sicily. Its setting is picturesque, and although the little town is not particularly elegant or exciting, it's a cheery place in the tourist season, with superb views of Taormina and the Sicilian hills. An archaeological park gives the town some cultural interest.

Most of what Giardini Naxos has to offer can be seen by taking a stroll along the long seafront road. Here you can book a boat trip, relax on the sand, rent your own boat, admire the views, swim or enjoy a meal at one of the many sea-view restaurants. Look out for a couple of Roman granite columns, which were discovered in the sea nearby. Most of the tourist businesses are at the southern end of the town, where you'll find a cluster of hotels and Giardini Naxos's widest stretch of beach.

Here you'll find a choice of nicely-presented beach establishments where you can rent sunbeds or eat at the attached restaurants and bars. Before choosing your preferred *lido*, compare their atmosphere and offerings as well as their prices; some are smarter than others, and they may offer different features such as a little children's playground. There is also plenty of free-access beach along the waterfront, though most of the beach is narrow and not necessarily as clean as the private areas.

For many, the resort's attractions are the beach and the proximity to Taormina, combined with cheaper accommodation prices. But the town does have a handful of sights of its own as well. If you're staying in Giardini Naxos, you may find it interesting to visit the historic Castello di Schisò, towards the port at the southern end of town. Once a fortress defending the settlement on this headland, it later became a base for the sugar-processing industry and then an aristocratic home, and is now being restored and opened to the public by a cultural association. At the time of writing just a few rooms and the courtyard can be visited (admission charge); these are mildly interesting, and include a long chamber which was once, before it was enclosed, the rampart along the battlements. The courtyard is an appealingly decrepit and evocative spot, with the ruins of the sugar-processing buildings on one side and cats sneaking through broken doorways. In an internal room look out for the Romanesque crosses carved into wooden beams.

Giardini Naxos may not seem remarkable now, but historically it's extremely important. It was the site, according to ancient writers, of the first Greek colony in Sicily, Naxos, established before other cities which are now better remembered: Syracuse, Agrigento, Selinunte. What is left of Greek Naxos can be visited in an archaeological park and museum at the southern end of the modern town on the headland called Capo Schisò. This was the site of the colonial city; an extensive site which was was used as farmland and not excavated properly until relatively recently, with excavations still under way.

It takes some time to follow paths through the site, and the ruins are not terribly dramatic compared with Sicily's more famous Greek sites. But the atmosphere and the green, rural surroundings, make this a pleasant place to wander and evoke the past. The sight of Etna rising above lemon trees, pines, grass and ruined walls is a dramatic one. Information boards around the site try to make some sense of the visible ruins but really the best thing to do is stroll and absorb the general atmosphere. Low ruined walls still define the layout of ancient thoroughfares and houses, and visitors can walk down a 'street'. The most substantial ruins are stretches of the city wall, with imposing stone gateways still in place.

To help see the site in context, visit the museum by the entrance before exploring. The museum presents information in Italian and English, and contains an interesting assortment of local finds, from pottery fragments to statuettes wearing the enigmatic archaic smile. A marble altar dedicated to the goddess Enyo with a script similar to that used in the Greek Cycladic islands has provided evidence of a connection between Sicilian Naxos and the Greek island Naxos, always said to have been the home of the earliest settlers who named this colony. Other interesting exhibits include a doll with jointed limbs from the 5th century BCE, an altar carved with two winged sphinxes and a bronze Thracian helmet decorated with hair and ears.

The archaeological park and museum are managed by the Parco Archeologico Naxos-Taormina, along with the Greek Theatre in Taormina and Isola Bella at Mazzaro. At the time of writing there are combined tickets for the park and Isola Bella. The site is open daily with hours varying through the year.

Out at the tip of the headland beyond the archaeological park is another little cluster of bar-restaurants. The town's pride in its ancient Greek origins can be seen everywhere : a sculpture trail of sculptures inspired by Greek mythology, including a statue of Nike, a little 'temple' construction and of course the 'Naxos' part of the placename.

The local tourist information office can be found next to Hotel La Riva, on the stretch of seafront between the port and the town's striking 20th-century church, Santa Maria Immacolata. This is a good place to pick up bus timetables and useful information for making the most of your stay.

Boat trips set off several times a day in season, organised by different companies, mostly from the port, with tours along the coast to Isola Bella and the local Grotta Azzurra (Blue Cave), allowing time for a brief dip in the sea. It's also possible to book coach excursions to see some of the inland sights in this part of Sicily.

Giardini Naxos isn't a particularly romantic or 'special' destination in itself. But it's an affordable alternative to the more elegant Taormina and has the advantage of its beachside setting. For a seaside holiday with easy access to sightseeing and transport, it's an option that will suit many travellers. As well as very local trips to Taormina, Castelmola and Mazzaro, it's also easy to plan trips further afield: to Etna, Catania and beyond, without the need to hire a car.

Giardini Naxos travel and transport

Giardini Naxos is on the eastern coast of Sicily, very close to Taormina. The most convenient airport is Catania. There are direct buses from the airport (also stopping in central Catania, with the final destination of Taormina). Services are run by Etna Trasporti/Interbus and are approximately hourly, with the journey taking an hour and fifteen minutes. There are several stops in Giardini Naxos, so check with your accommodation which stop you should request. Fares are cheap and timetables can be seen on the Interbus site. When staying in the resort you can use the same bus service or additional local Interbus services to reach Taormina, twenty minutes away.

Taormina and Giardini Naxos share a railway station, called Taormina-Giardini, on a line which runs down the coast of Sicily from Messina to Siracusa. The station is at the northern end of the long-strung out resort of Giardini Naxos and is a long walk from the tourist hub; again, if you're staying in town it's best to check with your hotel how far away it is and whether you should catch a bus or taxi with your luggage.

As well as the public bus services, there is also an open-top tourist bus which connects the resort with Taormina and Mazzaro, around the headland, and Castelmola up in the hills. This is an enjoyable way to travel and although it's expensive, you can get reasonable value from a 24-hour ticket if you plan your time well.

Walking between Taormina and Giardini Naxos

Energetic visitors might be interested in walking down to Giardini Naxos from Taormina. With a height difference of around 700ft between the two towns, this isn't an enterprise to undertake too lightly (and I wouldn't recommend climbing in the other direction). To walk from Taormina down towards the station and Giardini Naxos, start by taking Vicolo la Floresta, which leads south off Corso Umberto just to the north of Piazza IX Aprile. Heading down, the route is straightforward, with brick and stone underfoot to start off with but then becoming rougher underfoot as the path zigzags. At time of writing the route had been damaged by landslips after heavy rains (fairly common, particularly in autumn). The path was blocked by barriers, but determined walkers were bypassing these and negotiating the landslip. The route emerges on a road parallel to main coastal road. Walk five minutes to the right to reach the railway station, joining the main road on the way. It takes around half an hour to get down to the station then perhaps the same time again to head along the seafront as far as the tourist information office in Giardini Naxos.

Castelmola, a Taormina excursion

Castelmola, perched on a hilltop, is a good half-day excursion from Taormina, and with footpaths connecting the two, it offers a chance for some exercise to work off all those rich Sicilian meals. On a clear day the views down over Taormina, across the coast and towards Etna are fantastic.

Castelmola

Castelmola is a tiny, picturesque village perched on a craggy hilltop, above and slightly inland from Taormina. You can see it from Giardini Naxos and from some of Taormina's viewpoints, and if you don't mind some steep uphill sections, you can hike from Taormina to Castelmola and back. Many visitors, though will prefer the easier option of catching a public or tourist bus up to Castelmola, and then walking the attractive downhill route back to the larger resort. The village makes a very worthwhile outing, whether you walk, drive or bus.

From the wide piazza at the entrance to town, where buses turn, Castelmola is easily explored. Signposted uphill is the village's thirteenth-century castle, the Castello. Now in ruins, this fortress was dramatically situated to command the hills and valleys, so has wonderful views over the surrounding hills and coast.

Although it's small and doesn't have any major sights other than its ruined castle, Castelmola is an interesting and picturesque settlement, where a certain rugged authenticity mixes with tourist-oriented craft shops. The little streets and alleys are worth exploring before you make your way back down to Taormina: you'll find a surprisingly imposing Duomo and several smaller churches, including the Chiesa di San Giorgio (1450) which contains a charming little statue of St. George on his charger.

There is a choice of restaurants and cafés in Castelmola, and eating is a pleasant way to spend time here away from expensive and busy Taormina, so timing your visit around lunchtime is a good plan. An alternative is to pick up a picnic lunch from the general store along Via A. de Gasperi (which leads from Piazza San Antonio). You can have the rolls filled with local cheeses or meats, and sit down for a pleasant outdoors meal on the next stretch of the walk.

If you are of a robust disposition, one of the strangest sights of Castelmola is the historic Bar Turrisi and its phallic-themed décor. Celebrating in flamboyant style the ancient emblem of fertility and luck, and also the more risqué and libertine aspects of Taormina's history, the bar's interior is filled with penises in every medium and of every size, from large stone sculptures to the bathroom taps. The bar has balconies overlooking the pretty little village piazza, and serves granitas and almond wine, "elixir of love", which you can also buy in souvenir bottles (not all phallic-shaped) to take away.

Castelmola is a simple and gritty place in comparison with sybaritic Taormina. It's a picturesque and easy excursion, with the added bonus of an attractive footpath linking the two towns. Although close to Taormina and visited by tourists, it still feels worlds away from the crowded streets of the larger town.

With a few places to eat and drink, and a totally different, less touristy feel, Castelmola would be an unusual and atmospheric choice for an overnight stay. There are a few B&B and hotel options in and around the hilltop village, some of which have superb views. In the heart of the village is the Borgo Medievale B&B, with décor inspired by tales of King Arthur. Visitors should consider that the narrow mountain roads make it a tricky base for exploring by car, and the village is very small and quiet in the evenings especially out of season.

Walking between Castelmola and Taormina

It's possible to make the excursion from Taormina to Castelmola on foot, taking a circular route which climbs from Taormina to Castelmola, then descends by a different route with the option of including Taormina's Castello Saraceno, the ruined castle poised directly above Taormina. Note that footpaths around Taormina are occasionally damaged by heavy rainfall and landslips (especially after autumn storms), so I'd suggest checking your route with the tourist information office in Taormina before setting off.

The first section, Taormina to Castelmola, is the least inspiring stretch, with a big climb, so many visitors will prefer to skip the uphill workout and take a bus from Taormina to Castelmola, before enjoying the more attractive and leisurely walk downhill.

Taormina - Castelmola

From Porta Messina, head uphill and turn right past the fountain and archway. Follow Via Dietro Cappuccini. After a short stretch of road, you'll come to an unobtrusive set of steps on the left, Salita Branco, also signposted for Castelmola. Once an old mule-path, the concrete steps head upwards past the buildings of the local school. This climb is tiring and not particularly interesting, apart from the views back over the sea. Emerging on Via Branco, take the left hand bend, uphill.

When you reach the main road, cross over. Take the lane which continues upwards towards a cluster of houses. Following the small signs for Castelmola (with a pedestrian symbol) you'll find yourself on a path winding around to the right, under the crags on which the village sits. Looking back, you may see traces of the historic necropolis on the ridge - but you'll get a better view on the route back down. The steps are steep, so when you emerge into Castelmola's Piazza San Antonio you'll probably feel you deserve a long cold drink at the outdoor tables of the Bar San Giorgio.

Castelmola - Castello Saraceno - Taormina

Aim downhill from the area of the Duomo, and you should find yourself on a road wide enough for cars, curving around the base of the village. After a sharp bend, the pedestrian path to Taormina descends from this road, with a signpost to identify it. First port of call is the tiny Chiesa di San Biagio, which - according to the sign outside - dates back to the first century. Inside is a damaged eighteenth-century fresco.

Although money has been spent on this footpath at one point (hand rails, paved steps and lamp-posts), maintenance is evidently intermittent. The path is lovely, dropping through ancient agricultural terraces - mostly now overgrown with prickly pears and rampant wild flowers, which also quilt the grassy banks. A few intriguing cottages, semi-ruined, dot the slopes. After a picnic spot, as you approach a ridge, look upwards for a view of the necropolis: a rocky outcrop above, peppered with dark grave-openings. Shortly after this, the path passes through a ruined stone gateway. It finally descends in little steps to a narrow lane which you follow until it emerges onto a bend of via Leonardo da Vinci.

This path is called the Sentiero dei Saraceni. An old mule path connecting Taormina and Castelmola, it is said to have been used by the Saracens who besieged Taormina a thousand years ago. The ruined arch, a surviving part of ancient town defences, is known as the Porta dei Saraceni.

From this point you can either descend to Taormina, or continue with another climb up to the Castello Saraceno and the Santuario della Madonna della Rocca (see 'Things to do' page) above the town. To visit these other sights, continue for a short way along the main road to the left. Then a staircase on the left allows you to head straight uphill, cutting through the zigzagging streets. A stiff climb later, and you emerge on the spine of the ridge, by a bus stop on the main road. Cross over for the approach road for the Castello (which passes several bars and restaurants).

There are great views over Taormina from outside the chapel at the end of the lane, the Santuario della Madonna della Rocca. A path leads upwards to the castello entrance: however at the time of writing the ruins have been closed to the public for years. Back at the chapel, a long zigzag path leads back down to Taormina, past the traditional Stations of the Cross, offering plenty more panoramic photo-opportunities. You emerge on Via Circonvallazione, above Corso Umberto.

To miss this detour, and head straight on down into Taormina, head downhill around the bend in the road. You can simply follow the winding road around into the town centre, or head downhill through smaller streets, starting with a right turn onto Via Wilhelm Von Gloden and dropping to the left down the steps of Via Salita Celestina Penna, leading to Via Paterno di Biscari and then cutting to the right down Via della Chiusa or Vico Polibio. The route emerges onto a busier street (Via Diodoro Siculo/Via Apollo Arcageta), leading to the Porta Catania and Corso Umberto.

Porta Messina and Porta Catania

In ancient times Taormina was protected by a circuit of walls with a triple fortification system, which from the north on the side looking towards

Messina continued in a north-east direction and ended in the west on the side looking towards Catania. Traces of these walls can still be seen today not only in the centre of the town where the clock-tower stands, but also at the two furthest ends of the town where there are two entrances, commonly called Porta Messina and Porta Catania.

Porta Messina, restored at the beginning of the 19th century, was named Porta Ferdinanda when it was opened in 1808 by Ferdinand IV of Bourbon. There is a tablet commemorating the occasion on the top of its arch. Porta Catania on the other hand is the end result of various changes and restorations, the last of which were performed in 1440 by the Aragonese. The Aragonese coat-of-arms sculpted in relief above the city coat-of-arms in the centre on the top part of the gate.

The fountain in Piazza Duomo

Taormina's emblem. This Barocco style fountain, built in 1635, is in Taormina marble with three concentric steps at its base. On each of the fountain's four sides there are some small columns supporting basins; mythological ponies overlook the basins and fountain water flows out of their mouths.

The eastern base of this large fountain contains a fourth basin, larger than the others but no longer used since it was a watering-place for animals. There is a smaller octagonal basin in the middle of the fountain base with four putti resting on it; on the east side, two of these putti hold two smaller putti each, forming the base of an octagonal basin decorated with three seals showing their heads and tails.

Three mythological characters resembling Tritons stands in the middle of this latter basin with their arms crossed over their heads so as to support another basin decorated in low-relief; a round base inside this basin holds a basket of fruit on the top of which stands Taormina's coat-of-arms. The town's coat-of-arms normally pictures a male centaur but in this case it was turned into a female centaur and a two-footed one at that

The Byzantine Madonna

The Byzantine Madonna or "non hand-made" Madonna is now kept in the Cathedral of Taormina. This Madonna was found inside an old well and was probably placed there to save it from the many invasions and pillaging that went on during the Arabian era, although tradition has it that it was left there by the angels. That is why it is called the "non hand-made" Madonna, meaning not made by human hands. It is an oil painting on panel covered with a layer of silver and semiprecious stones. Unmistakably belonging to the Byzantine era, the painting was dedicated to Holy Mary of the Greeks.

The San Domenico

This Dominican monastery, now the San Domenico Hotel, was the third monastery in Taormina. Its origins and history are related to Damiano Rosso, a Dominican friar who was a descendant of the Altavilla family and Prince of Cerami; after becoming a friar he donated all he owned to the Dominican order in 1430.

His antique mansion was therefore turned into Taormina's Dominican monastery. The "San Domenico" was the first or perhaps the only castle existing in Taormina during the middle ages. Some centuries later the estate was given back to Damiano Rosso's heirs who turned it into a hotel. The only part of the former monastery to remain open to worship was the chapel which, however, was destroyed by bombings on July 9, 1943.

The congress hall of the hotel was built on the ruins of the chapel, conserving the remains of the minor altars. The bombings did not damage the rest of the hotel nor the 50 cells which were later turned into luxurious hotel-rooms. The beautiful cloister and magnificent park, which overlook the sea and have a view of Mount Etna, are the most charming parts of the hotel. A second wing, added to the hotel in the 1930s, harmoniously reflects the architectural style of the rest of the building with many authentic art treasures as well as sacred vestments and vessels and paintings by well-known artists.

The Clock Tower

The clock-tower acts as an entrance gate to the part of the town that historians call "the 15th century area". Dating back to the 12th century, the tower was razed to the ground during a French invasion under Louis XIV in 1676. What can be admired today is a reconstruction by the people of Taormina in 1679, who added a large clock to the tower.

Studies carried out over the years, however, have shown that the foundations of the tower in large square bricks of Taormina stone date back further than the first construction date of the tower. It can therefore be supposed that the first tower was built on the ruins of an older defence wall which would have dated back to the origins of the town, in other words the 4th century B.C.

The Gymnasium (The Naumachie)

The Gymnasium in Taormina was in the area called "Giardinazzo", where the so-called Naumachiae ruins can still today be seen. The "Gymnasium" was usually a construction with a rectangular perimeter, surrounded on its four sides by an arcade supported by columns. The clearing in the centre was for games and gymnastical exercises. In fact, it was the place where young men were educated from both a civil-religious and operative point of view. The athletes who participated in the Olympic Games were trained in the Gymnasia.

In Taormina the only remaining wall of the antique Gymnasium rests on a double row of well-cut steps in Taormina stone which form the base of the wall. There are 18 niches with round arches and 18 other smaller rectangular niches. The name "Naumachiae" (from Greek meaning "sea battle") improperly given to these ruins is probably attributable to the fact that there is a large reservoir on the remaining wall, which used to be a water supply for the Gymnasium and a reserve for the whole town.

The Public Gardens

The town gardens, named after the Duke of Cesarò who was a representative of Taormina's constituency when they were made, were donated by the Cacciola-Trevelyan family during the 1920s. Inside, there is a thick vegetation and a typically Mediterranean array of hedges and flower-beds with cobbled paths which lengthwise connect the almost three hectares of park. An avenue lined with olive-trees in memory of the fallen during various wars runs among precious trees of various species, some of which are rare and extraordinarily beautiful.

In the centre and on the north-east end of the gardens, there are some characteristic pagoda-style towers with arabesque designs, made of bricks and edged with lavic pumice-stone. Florence Trevelyan, an English nobelwoman, had these towers built so as to study the birds since the was a keen ornithologist. Relics from the two World Wars are on show in a few clearings and a war monument to the fallen can be seen near the natural "Teatro di Verzura" (Greenery Theatre)

The Arabian Necropolis

Just a few hundred metres away from the town's northern gate, along the road that from Capo Taormina leads up to the centre of the town, the Arabian necropolis, even though it is defined as Byzantine by many, is rare evidence of the "daily" aspects of that period.

It is thought to have been created during the 10th and 11th centuries and is defined as a columbary necropolis due to the fact that the cells are symmetrical and situated one on top of the other. What can be seen today are the remains of a much larger construction which went on towards the north-eastern part of the town centre between the current necropolis site and the lower Church of St. Peter outside the town walls.

Greek Theater of Taormina

One of Sicily's most celebrated sites is the ancient Greco-Roman theater in Taormina. The impressive ruins rest on the hillside over the sea, renowned as much for its incredible condition as its panoramic position. The ancient structure is still in use - it hosts operas, concerts and the annual Taormina Film Festival.

The theater was built by the Greeks who excavated the hillside to take advantage of the natural slope for seating, taking in the breathtaking view of Mt. Etna. The remains of a small temple can seen next to it, and there was also a colonnade that led to it. The theater was enlarged by the Romans when they conquered the island. The 120-meter diameter structure is the second largest in Sicily, after the Greco-Roman theater in Siracusa.

It is justifiably one of Sicily's most visited attractions, drawn to the history, the condition of the remains and the stunning setting. You can see the sapphire waters below, the town of Taormina, and the smoking heights of Mt. Etna from here. It is more than the worth the €8 entrance price just to enjoy the postcard-perfect panoramas!

Parco Fluviale dell'Alcantra

North of Etna is a regional park that follows the 50 kilometer water course of the Alcantara River. A unique and geologically interesting zone, the river cuts through low rocks and deeper gorges, creating a beautiful fluviale landscape.

There are park offices in both Francavilla di Sicilia and Castiglione di Sicilia, with trails along the river, which eventually empties into the sea south of Taormina. Along the way it cuts through ancient clay deposits, modeled into sculptural forms, magma flows, and basalt canyons created from lava.

There are cascades, plants and animals in the park, and refreshing walks along the cool river, with a dip in one of the natural pools, is certainly refreshing in the hot summer

Isola Bella

Isola Bella is, like the name implies, a pretty island. The tiny isle is part of the municipality of Taormina. Is is so charming that it is often called "the pearl of the Ionian".

The rocky island was once the property of King Ferdinand II, who gifted it to the city of Taormina in 1806. It went through a series of private owners, and a picturesque villa was built on the summit of the island's hill taking in both the spectacular sea views as well as the coastline and mountains. It was obtained by the Region of Sicily in 1990 and turned into a nature reserve. There is an abundance of birds and some rare lizards found here.

Isola Bella is connected to the beaches of the mainland by a pathway. At low tide it widens and so the island almost appears to be part of the coast. The pebble beach on the island is prized for its protected location, sitting in the bay it is cuddled by the island and the mountains, giving it calm water and a longer bathing season as it escapes the winds and colder waves.

There are no services on Isola Bella, but the mainland beaches offer restaurants, cafes and entertainment. A stroll to the island and around its rocky perimeter is a must when you're in the area for the views and the unique atmosphere!

Aviary on Isola Bella

The elegant isle in Lake Maggiore known as Isola Bella has received some new residents in keeping with old traditions. The splendid gardens of the private island, owned by the noble Borromeo family, have always been a showcase for beauty, including an aviary built in the 1700s for rare canaries and parrots. The gardens have retained their splendor while the aviary fell into decline. But now, the Prince Borromeo (yes, the island and palace are still in the family's hands) have restored and repopulated it to colorful glory with more than a hundred of the feathered beauties. There are also rare white peacocks roaming the grounds.

The aviary is located in the Oriental Garden, but the park of this magical isle includes an Italian

Garden, an "agrumi" (citrus grove), a "pyramid" of terraces festooned with plants and statues, artistically designed and manicured box hedges, and more. It is a must-see when you're on Lake Maggiore! And now, with the pretty birds and white peacocks, it's even more magical than before!

Wunderbar

Cafe Wunderbar is Taormina's historic gathering spot. The cafe sits on the Piazza IX Aprile and has served literary and glitterati types for a century. Popularized by the likes of Greta Garbo, Oscar Wilde, Tennessee Williams and Elizabeth Taylor, it is still the "in" place for a drink or dolce in an elegant setting.

Grab a table on the piazza to watch the town's people parade or a spot on the panoramic terrace behind to take in the sweeping views of the sea while enjoying a refreshing granita or the island's famous cannoli. They are also known for the fruit-dotted cassata cake and their cocktails.

Monuments

The Greek-Roman Theatre

Is it Greek or Roman? This is a question that has always been open to debate among experts and critics. All their disputes would end if they remembered Taormina's origins as a Greek "Polis" and the fact that each and every ancient Greek town had its own Theatre where they performed tragedies by Aeschylus, Sophocles and Euripides and comedies by Aristophanes, just to name the most famous authors.

The Theatre in Taormina is the second-largest in Sicily after the one in Siracusa. All the Romans did later, in accordance with their well-known ostentatious nature, was enlarge the theatre as it was very small. And it apparently took decades to build. It is fifty metres wide, one hundred and twenty metres long and twenty metres high, which means that about 100,000 cubic metres of stone had to be removed. Further evidence that the Theatre is of Greek origin is in the well-cut bricks of Taormina stone (similar to marble) below the scene of the Theatre; these are a typical example of the ancient Greek building technique.

The theatre is divided into three main sections: the scene, the orchestra and the cavea. The scene is opposite the cavea and is obviously where the actors used to perform. There is now a large ten-metre long portion missing in the centre of the scene, supposedly caused by attacks during the wars. This serious damage to the theatre makes it nevertheless even more evocative due to the magnificent panorama (the bay of Naxos and Mount Etna) which can now be seen.

According to reconstructions by experts, the scene was decorated with two series of columns of the Corinthian order, recognizable due to the shape of the capitals and their acanthus leaf design; the acanthus is a wild Mediterranean plant. The orchestra of the theatre was the flat clearing in the centre which separated the scene from the cavea. This area was for the musicians, but the choruses and dancers also performed there.

The word "orchestra", nowadays meaning a musical band, comes from this part of the Greek theatre. The cavea on the other hand is the series of steps, from the lowest to the highest ones at the top, where the spectators were seated. The first and last semicircular steps were 62 and 147.34 metres long respectively. The steps were carved out of the rock and, in places where there was none, they were built in masonry.

The theatre is thought to have been able to seat about 5,400 spectators. No one is sure of when the Theatre was actually erected. Those who believe it was built by the Greeks say it must have been around the middle of the third century B.C., when Hiero was the tyrant of Siracusa. But due to the theatre's structural characteristics, some say it was erected by Roman engineers to be used exclusively by the Greeks.

This would explain all the Greek inscriptions inside the theatre. Nowadays the ancient Theatre is still one of Taormina's main attractions. As it is still practicable, the theatre seated the audiences of the most important Italian cinematographic event, the "David di Donatello" award, for many years; now an international festival entitled "Taormina Arte", lasting the whole summer period, is held there with cinema, theatre, ballet and symphonic music reviews.

Badia Vecchia

As in the case of Palazzo Duca di S. Stefano, Badia Vecchia was purchased by the Municipality of Taormina in 1960 for 12 million lire. It was at first restored but then abbandoned once again and left to the mercy of vandals. Armando Dillon, a Neopolitan architect, is of the opinion that this building was called Badia Vecchia due to the fact that it was at one stage the home of Mother Abbess Euphemia, who was a regent of the Kingdom of Sicily from 1355 in the name of her younger brother Frederic IV, known as "the Simple".

But this is only a theory, even though it is a suggestive one. It does seem, however, that the mansion is called Badia Vecchia because it once was an abbey. This theory is based on the discovery of a sacred painting at the bottom of a rain-water well and it seems that the painting was hidden there so as to save it from one of the many invasions on Taormina.

And all the niches inside were then thought to be niches for icons and not just simple storage spaces. The Gothic architecture of Badia Vecchia is very similar to that of Palazzo Duca di S. Stefano. It therefore follows that the two buildings are of the same period, in other words, the late 1300s. The Gothic style of this building too is therefore influenced by Arabian and Norman art. Badia Vecchia is formed by three rooms having the same surface area. A frieze of inlaid lavic stone and white Siracusa stone decorates the building, marking the dividing line between the first and second floors.

Three magnificent mullioned windows rest on the frieze one beside the other so that they resemble a single window with six openings. The ogival arches decorating the side windows have a single rosette while the ogival-arched central window has three. The top of all the facades of Badia Vecchia is decorated with swallow-tailed merlons, making it resemble a fortress-like tower. Badia Vecchia, like Palazzo Duca di S. Stefano, was built as a stronghold along the boundary walls, the former to protect the northern part of the town and the latter the southern part.

Palazzo Corvaja

The Arabian dominion in Sicily lasted from the 9th to the 11th century and the Moslems remained in Taormina in particular from the year 902 to 1079. During the 11th century the Arabs reinforced the town's defences by building, among other things, a tower which is really the main part of today's Palazzo Corvaja.

The cubic tower reminded the Arabs of their sacred "Al Ka 'bah" which, according to Mahomet, was the first tempie erected to God by Abraham at the Mecca. The tower was extended at the end of the 13th century with the addition of the area which is on the left of the entrance portal. Together with this new wing, a staircase was built leading from the courtyard to the first floor.

And on the landing there are three magnificent panels in Siracusa stone scuplted in high-relief: the first one pictures the creation of Eve; the second panel, the originai sin; and the third is of the expulsion of Adam and Eve from Paradise. The right wing of the building was constructed at the beginning of the 1400s in order to house the meetings of the Sicilian Parliament which were held, the first in 1411, in the large 15th century hall in the presence of Queen Bianca of Navarra, regent of the Kingdom of Sicily.

And for this same reason Palazzo Corvaja is also called Parliament House or the Palace of Queen Bianca of Navarra. In any case the mansion is named after the Corvaja family, one of the oldest and most noble families in Taormina. The men of the family have been renowned in the administration of the town as well as in arts and magistrature. Palazzo Corvaja was in a pitiful state of total neglect with several families living there at the one time until the end of the Second World War in 1945.

That same year the first mayor of Taormina had the building dispossessed and Armando Dillon, a Neopolitan architect, restored it all from 1945 until 1948. In 1960 Palazzo Corvaja was enlarged and the new wing now houses the offices of the "Servizio Turistico Regionale", the Tourist Office. Near the Odeon, just a few steps away from the Zecca, near the old entrance to the Naumachiae and not far from the Greek-Roman Theatre, Palazzo Corvaja is certainly one of Taormina's historical landmarks.

As regards the architectural style of the building, it is a mixture of styles due to the different eras during which it was built and extended. Its styles go from Arabian to Norman to Gothic. The battlements of the tower are Arabian and are formed by a double row of square holes surmounted by small merlons. The mullioned windows of the 14th century hall are Gothic. This type of window in Gothic architecture is divided by a small column so as to create two entrances for the light. The 15th century hall, where the Sicilian Parliament meetings were held, is all in Norman style.

The Antiquarium

The Antiquarium is a small archeological museum on show in two rooms of the Antique Theatre guardian's house, once called the House of the Englishmen because it was supposedly inhabited by English families during the first days of tourism in Taormina. Few archaeological specimens remain in this house-museum since most of them are now in Naples, Messina and Siracusa.

One of the most interesting things is a large square block of Taormina marble, formerly the base of a statue. On the front of this base an inscription reads "The Tauromenitani (the Taormina people) dedicate this statue to Olympio, winner of the horse race in the games at Olympia", evidence that Taormina had a winner at the Olympic Games. This statue base was found in 1770 while extension work was being carried out in the "S. Maria del Valverde" monastery, which is now a Carabineri post in Vittorio Emanuele (Badia) square.

Another statue base in Taormina marble, according to the inscription on it, was dedicated to Caius Claudius Marcellus, Propraetor of Sicily in the year 77 B.C. A 1.75 metre pillar in Taormina marble, discovered in 1864, is called the "Tavola degli Strateghi" (Table of the Strategists), a slab engraved with the names of the strategists, who were not soldiers but those in charge of administering justice in Taormina. Another pillar is the "Tavola dei Ginnasiarchi" (Table of the Gymnasiarchs), magistrates in charge of the Gymnasium where the young men were educated psychologically and physically.

There is also an interesting small oval sarcophagus in marble, probably made for a child. It is sculpted externally in high-relief with Baccanal scenes involving children. The sarcophagus was discovered in 1839 in the gardens of what was then a Franciscan Friary, now a nursing home run by the Franciscan Missionaries of Mary. Some stone bricks can also be seen, the top surfaces of which are lapped and engraved with financial statements of the Polis. These were found in 1833 at the base of the Greek-Roman Theatre. Therefore in Taormina, as in Rome and Athens, documents related to the political, civil and financial system of the town were conserved "for eternity" as they were engraved on stone.

The Odeon

There are no doubts as to the origins of the Odeon, or "small theatre". It was built directly by the Romans when Taormina became a military colony in the year 21 B.C. under Caesar Augustus Octavian, the first Roman emperor. Much smaller than the other theatre, it is evidence of how important culture was to Taormina in those days.

The small theatre is just behind a hill named after St. Catherine of Alexandria in Egypt, near Palazzo Corvaja. It was found accidentally on June 5th 1892 and until that moment no one had even suspected it existed. The story of its discovery is an unusual one. A blacksmith named Antonio Bambara was digging in his land behind St. Catherine's Church when his pick uncovered a red brick construction. A year later the real excavations began and the Odeon appeared, badly damaged in various sections. The architecture of the Roman Odeon is almost identical to that of the larger theatre. The monument is oriented differently.

In fact the Greek-Roman Theatre faces the south while the small Odeon faces north-east. It was built with lateritious material, in other words with large clay bricks joined together with lime. The Odeon has the same construction plan as all other

Roman theatres and is divided into three main sections: the scene, the orchestra and the cavea.

The scene of the Odeon consisted of the stylobate (base) and the peristyle (colonnade) of a Greek temple, some say dedicated to Aphrodite, which was discovered during the excavations on the Odeon. Apart from theatrical performances, this small Odeon, built right in the centre of the Polis, is thought to have been used for musical recitals and auditions reserved to magistrates, important civil, military and religious people and their families as well as to guests of consequence.

Palazzo Duca di S. Stefano

The palace's square structure, massiveness, position and battlemented walls make it look like a fortress, therefore making people think that the initial constructor was a Norman. This 13th century palace, situated near Porta Catania, has a beautiful garden in front of its main facades facing east and north and was the home of the De Spuches, a noble family of Spanish origin, who were Dukes of S. Stefano di Brifa and Princes of Galati, two towns on the Jonian coast in the Messina area.

Palazzo Duca di S. Stefano is surely one of the masterpieces of Sicilian Gothic art, in which the elements of Arabian and Norman art merge. Arabian reminiscences are aroused by the decoration on the top part of the palace: a wide frieze runs along the east and north facades formed by a wavy decoration in lavic stone alternated with rhombus-shaped inlays in white Siracusa stone, together forming a magnificent lace of marquetry.

Norman art instead is recalled by its square tower-like plan and by what remains of the swallow-tailed merlons on the top of the building. The

Palace is made up of three square overlapping sections. The entrance to the ground floor is an ogival arch constructed with squared bricks of black basalt (lavic stone) and white granite (Taormina stone). The first floor was reached by means of drawbridges and moving staircases through the small door which can still today be seen between the two mullioned windows on the first floor.

An internal staircase, made entirely of wood, was reproduced when the building was restored, in the 18th century. On the second floor there are four beautiful windows indisputably in Gothic style, two facing east and two facing north, the noble prospects of the palace. The four mullioned windows have an elaborate structure with rosettes and small trilobe arches as well as triple cordons framing the ogival arches. A column of pink granite stands in the middle of the ground floor and is thought to have once been in the Greek Theatre.

In the gardens overlooked by the noble facades there is a well for the collection of rain-water (a puteal) which was the water supply for the whole palace. The municipality of Taormina only gained possession of Palazzo Duca di S. Stefano in 1964 when it was bought for 64 million lire (about € 33.000,00) from Vincenzo De Spuches, a young descendant of the De Spuches family, who lived in Palermo.

Palazzo Duca di S. Stefano today houses the Mazzullo Foundation, run by a clever sculptor who has succeeded in turning tradition into modernness. Many of his sculptures are on show in the palace. It is a location for civil weddings and temporary exibitions

Palazzo Ciampoli

Palazzo Ciampoli is the most recent of the mediaeval mansions in Taormina, since its origin dates back to the beginning of the 15th century. The year in which this splendid mansion was built was 1412 and the coat-of-arms above its main entrance portal bears this date.

In 1926 the "Palazzo Vecchio" Hotel was built in the gardens of Palazzo Ciampoli and architecturally the hotel vaguely recalled the famous "Palazzo Vecchio" or "Palazzo della Signoria" in Florence. Until a few years ago, Palazzo Ciampoli housed one of Taormina's most famous night clubs, "Sesto Acuto", named after the ogival arches which ornate the building according to the Gothic style that it recalls. Since two coats-of-arms, one with a shield and a flag, the other with a shield and three stars, can be found in both Palazzo Ciampoli and Palazzo Corvaja, the former is thought to have been owned by the Corvaja family before being passed on to the Ciampoli family.

The only noticeable part of Palazzo Ciampoli is its front prospect resting on a set of wide and steep steps which act as its natural base. Originally there was a large open courtyard in front of the building but all that remains of it today is a round-arched portal with its base in Taormina marble and two bas-reliefs of the heads of roman emperors in the corners above the arch. The mansion was hit and destroyed by bombings in 1943. The above-mentioned portal, however, was later reconstructed with the same marble slabs that had collapsed.

The Catalan architecture in Palazzo Ciampoli is easily recognized. In fact the structure of the building has Spanish characteristics: in its short northern prospect there is a single window whose arch is outlined by an architrave-panel with lobes connected to form festoons sculptured all along it. The top of its main prospect is ornated with small triangular merlons which, however, are not as majestic as the swallow-tailed merlons to be found on the other mediaeval constructions in Taormina

Piazza Ix Aprile In Taormina

The square is known for the breathtaking view of the azure Ionian Sea and of the Mount Etna.

Lined with pricey cafés and brimming with visitors and caricature artists, it's the best place to sit back with a cappuccino and enjoy the relaxed resorty ambience of Taormina.

The square was named after the 9th of April, 1860, when mass in the Taormina cathedral down the street was interrupted to announce that Garibaldi had landed at Marsala (on the far side of the island) to begin his conquest of Sicily that made it part of Italy

Actually, the news proves false. In fact Garibaldi landed at Marsala exactly one month later, on 9 May 1860. However, the inhabitants of Taormina wanted to recall that date dedicating the most beautiful square.

Saracen Castle In Taormina

The Saracen Castle (Castello saraceno) is situated in an elevated position above Taormina, at about 397m high.

Most probably it was the site of the antique acropolis of the Greek town of Taormina. The Romans and later the Byzantines must have strengthened the site. In 902 AD the town fell to the Muslims after a siege of 2 years. They rebuilt the castle into its present form with a trapezoid plan adapted to the shape of the rock and crenellated walls.

You can get to the castle via a staircase that starts from the *church of the Madonna della Rocca* climbs up to reach the door.

The remains of this fortification are constituted by the imposing tower, the walls on which is implanted a tower, a cistern and an underground corridor.

Today, The castle is unfortunately closed and can not be visited by those tourists who would like to see the wonder of this ancient historic monument and the magnificent panorama from the summit of Mount Tauro.

Fountain Piazza Duomo In Taormina

On the square, just in front of the Cathedral, is situated the fountain of Piazza Duomo.

The fountain was built in 1635 in the Baroque style, is also called "4 fountains" because the 4 small columns supporting basins which are located at the corners of the central basin; mythological ponies overlook the basins and fountain water flows out of their mouths.

The central part consists of two basins.

Above the two centrak basins, there is the Minotaur, half human and half horse, which is the emblem of the city of Taormina. Depicted in the female version, it has two arms holding an orb and scepter, symbols of power.

Churches

The Duomo
The fortress Duomo, which is what Taormina's main cathedral is considered, was built around the year 1400 on the ruins of a small mediaeval church. The Duomo has a Latin-cross plan with

three aisles; there are six minor altars in the two side aisles. The nave is held up by six monolithic columns, three on each side, in pink Taormina marble and their capitals have a foil and fish-scale decoration. The ceiling of the nave has wooden beams supported by carved corbels reproducing Arabian scenes with a Gothic air. The very interesting main portal was rebuilt in 1636 and has a large Renaissance-inspired rosette sculpted on it.

St. Pancra's Church

The church consecrated to the Patron of Taormina, St. Pancras, Bishop and martyr, was built on the ruins of a Greek temple dedicated to Jupiter Serapis. Parts of the temple's cell can still be seen in the southern wall of the church. This church is in Barocco style and dates back to the second part of the 16th century. Its main portal is very interesting with jambs and architraves in Taormina stone; two Ionian columns decorate each side of the portal.

Inside the church the intermediate floor with the organ can be seen above this portal.

Two interesting oil paintings on canvas hang above the two minor altars on the right of the church, one picturing the torture of St. Nicone and the other the consecration of St. Maximus who was St. Pancras' successor. Between the other two minor altars on the left of the church there is a fresco picturing Teofano Cerameo, Taormina's last Bishop during the 11th century. A low railing in wrought iron separates the rest of the church from the main altar which is lavishly decorated with polichrome marble slabs and an Ionian column on each side, like those on the external portal. There are eight angels on the altar, four on each side, and a bust of God giving his blessing. A fresco picturing the torture of St. Pancras can be seen on the right of the main altar.

St. Catherine's Church

The exact construction date of this church, consecrated to St. Catherine of Alexandria in Egypt and located in the centre of the town opposite Palazzo Corvaja, is not known. It is thought to date back to 1663, the year engraved on the tablet of the ossuary found outside the church and now located in the wall beside the staircase which leads to the crypt. The entrance door to the sacresty is on the left of the portal; the sacresty is thought to have been built before the Church, i.e. during the 16th century.

The facade of the sacresty is decorated with two small windows ornated with sea shells, the same decoration used on the architrave of its door. As it was built on the ruins of the Odeon, the remains of which can be seen behind the church, part of the orchestra and scene were destroyed. The scene of the Odeon is believed to have been created using the colonnade of a pre-existent Greek temple dedicated to Aphrodite.

St. George's Church

St. George's Anglican Church was built in the early 1920s on the iniziative of a small group of English people who used to spend most of the year in Taormina. The church was designed by Sir Harry Triggs, an English architect and the son-in-law of Sir Edward Hill, who owned the land and was a real promoter of Taormina's wonders. There are two aisles inside the church, which is divided by three round arches in Siracusa stone with two central columns as their base. The most beautiful part of the church is its large polichrome window behind the main altar picturing Jesus on the cross with St. Catherine on the left and St. George in his mediaeval armour on the right.

St. Augustine's Church

The Church of St. Augustine, nowadays known as the town library, was built towards the end of the 15th century by the people of Taormina and is said to have been originally devoted to St. Sebastian who had worked a miracle and saved the town by keeping the plague away. The Augustinian fathers later arrived in Taormina, took over and enlarged the church, turning it into a monastery; it then lost its St. Sebastian title and was named after St. Augustine.

The church, with its tie-beam cieling, has four niches on each side decorated with false Corinthian arches and columns. Originally decorated in late Sicilian Gothic style, the church was radically transformed around the year 1700 when the large ogival arch of the main portal was replaced by an architrave in Taormina stone. All that remains of the originai facade is a small rosette and the top of the ogival arch of the old portal.

Shrine To Our Lady Of The Fortress
Situated on the top of Mount Tauro, the Santuario Madonna della Rocca has perhaps one of the most beautiful and suggestive panoramas in Taormina. The shrine was built in 1640, taking advantage of the rock structure which forms a grotto there, and is still today one of the tourists' favourite sightseeing attractions.

Foods and Wine
Sicilian cuisine is deeply cosmopolitan, drawing from the culinary culture of all its invaders. The Arabs introduced aubergines and rice as well as a sweet and spicy cuisine. The French and Spanish refined the raw ingredients and the end result is a sumptuous Mediterranean stew in which pasta,

tomatoes, vegetables, sea food, lemons extra virgin olive oil and various herbs predominate.

Primarily, Sicilian food mixes Italian staples pasta, tomato souce and fresh vegetables with local specialities and products of the traditional island industries: red chillies, tuna, swordfish and sardines, olives, pine nuts and capers all figure heavily.

The mild winter climate and long summer mean that fruit and vegetables are less seasonal here than in northern Europe and are also much bigger and more impressive.

In Sicily you may discover the true "cucina povera", the pillar of the famous Mediterranean diet: pasta (fresh and dried) dressed with pure, extra virgin olive oil and fresh vegetables, lightly grilled fish, lamb or goat seasoned with herbs. A healthy, peasant food, unspoilt by cloying sauces: you will discover how well and how healthfully you can eat without heavy sauces and fats.

Taormina has approximately 80 restaurants, trattorie and pizzerie, all open from noon to 3 pm and from 7 until 12 pm or even later than that.

Although a trattoria is a cheaper, simpler place than a ristorante, in reality in Taormina they are both serving fabolous Sicilian meals.

Most ristoranti and trattorie in town display a menu outside with prices so that you know exactly what to expect.

Hors d'Oeuvres ("Antipasti"): Literally "before the meal". Starters in Taormina's restaurants are often sumptuously displayed to tempt you the minute you walk in: cold dishes as "insalata di mare" (seafood salad tossed in olive oil, lemon and herbs), vegetables, salami, ham, olives, stuffed artichoke hearths, anchovies and aubergines in various guises, "peperonata" (peppers in oil) or "pomodori ripeni" (stuffed tomatoes). Aubergines are a staple, wether grilled, fried, stuffed ("involtini di melanzane"), or baked in a cheese and tomato sauce ("melanzane alla parmigiana"). Or try "pesce spada affumicato", smoked swordfish or "alici marinate" (marinated anchovies).

A favourite starter is also "caponata", a dish of fried peppers, aubergines, tomatoes, courgettes and olives.

First course ("primo"): Soups or pasta dishes. In Taormina we recommend to try: Pasta with fresh tomatoes and basil, "pennette alla norma" (an eggplant sauce), "pasta con le sarde" (with a sauce of sardines, tomatoes, pine nuts and rasins), or "linguine al limone", surprisingly simple and delicious. Or "risotto alla marinara" (steamed rice with fresh seafood), "spaghetti al nero di seppia" (with the black squid sauce), "spaghetti ai frutti di mare" (seafood) or "spaghetti ai ricci di mare" (with sea-urchin's eggs).

Main courses ("secondi"): *Pesce (fish):* in Taormina you mustn't miss out "involtini di pesce spada" (grilled sword-fish rolls) and the "grigliata mista", a mixed seafood grill. Two other special treats in town are "triglie" (red mullets) and "aragosta" (the clawless Mediterranean lobster). "Sarde a beccafico" (filetted sardines stuffed with cheese, garlic, parsley and capers) or "neonata a pastelle" (tiny fried fish). *Carne (meat):* try the tasty local "salsiccia" (sausages in red wine with fennel seeds), "coniglio alla cacciatora" (rabbit steamed in herbs) or "capretto al forno" (baked kid batter).

Desserts: "Cassata" or "torta cassata" is an ice cream or tart with almonds and candied fruits, "cannoli alla ricotta" (sponge cake filled with a delicious cream made of sheep-milk and candied fruits), "sfogliatelle" (sweet ricotta turnovers), "paste di mandorla" (almond cakes) or "marzapane" (marchpane). "Gelato" (ice-cream) made in Taormina is simply unique and of course, granita, the typical Sicilian breakfast, especially in summer.

Wines: Italy ist the largest wine-producing country in the world. The south is more prodigious a producer of wine than the north and Sicily produces some of the best wines in the country. So once in Taormina we recommend to try:

Surrunding Areas

Alì Terme: 27 Km (16 miles) north of Taormina on the Ionian coast between Scaletta Zanclea and Nizza di Sicilia is the hydrothermal resort of Alí Terme: water and mud treatments suitable for chronic arthropathies, skin complaints, gynecological problems and inflammation of the respiratory system are available here. There are two spas: Granata Cassibile and Marino,

respectively using the waters and muds of five and two springs. The water temperature varies between 28 and 46° C. They are rich in boric acid, sulphur, sodium bromide, chloride, iodide and carbonic acid.

Easy to reach, a treatment here is also good for your health with the added attraction of a beach, archaeological sites and beautiful coastal and hill scenery nearby.

Antillo: In the Montagna Grande range of the southern Peloritan mountains, its history is bound to that of Savoca and the and the inhabitants are given over to agriculture and stock farming.

Casalvecchio Siculo: It lies in the southern Peloritan mountains on the south eastern slopes of

Mt. Sant'Elia. The village has Arab origins and was mentioned in 1130 as Calabiet, part of the feudal lands of the town of Savoca and until 1812 it belonged to the bishops of Messina. ….. From 1928 to 1939 Casalvecchio the abolished commune was joined to the town of that of Santa Teresa di Riva. The inhabitants devote themselves to primary activities. The main church (Sant'Onofrio) with a baroque facade houses an Epiphany by G. Camarda (1626), a precious marble after and, in the treasury, a statue of the saint in embossed silver and a 17th C. chalice. Nearby, on the left bank of the Agrò river rises a national monument, the church of saints Pietro e Paolo, of Basilian origin, rebuilt in 1172 by the master builder Gerardo il Franco.Running along the outer walls, in alternate layers of red bricks, black lava stones and wite limestone are slim pilaster strips, connected to intertwining pointed arches, crowned by crenellated work. The interior has three naves with semi-circular apses, the center one being rectangular.

Castelmola: Castelmola is a small medieval town perched on a mountain-peak overlooking Taormina and lies about 550 mts (1580 ft) above the sea level offering a magnificent view of the sea, Taormina, the coast of Calabria and Mt. Etna.

It counts slightly more than 1000 inhabitants. Very famous for the production of almond-wine and embroidery. The town center has two churches, the Mother Church which is a hodgepodge of architectural styles, and the Church of St. George, which dates from 1450 and is noted for its bell-tower. St. George's day, april 23, is a popular attraction for people who enjoy patronal festivals.

Many places are to be visited, such as the Spanish castle (14th century) or the St. Antonio square, the "belvedere" (scenic point), the Cathedral and all the typical medieval narrow alleys of the town. Mountains, hills and valleys beyond Castelmola abound with wild flowers, shrubs and trees and landscape is particularly scenic.

Castiglione Di Sicilia: Small town of very old origin, dominates the beautiful valley of Alcantara from above its rock. The town gets its name from "Castel Leone" which rises on the grindstone where 730 years b.c. an observation point was erected by the Greeks. In the following centuries Normans, Swabians and Arabs each brought new culture and costumes. Today Castiglione offers a urban plan of great interest, original embroidery, excellent red wine and savory gastronomic delicacies (very good are the noodles whit nettle).

Castroreale: This village was probably founded by the Siculans in the 8th C. B.C. It immediately became of strategic importance for its position controlling the Milazzo valley. For this reason, during the centuries, the town was granted with generous privileges by several kings and was always quite rich.

The church of the Assunta flanked by a 16th century bell tower, houses a statue of Saint Cathrine made in 1534 by Antonello Gagini, also responsible for the "Annunciation" dated 1519 to be admired in the church of Saint Agata. In the church of Santa Maria del Gesù is the tomb of Geronimo Rosso again by A. Gagini.

Every 23/25th of August, great celebrations are held when a crucifix 12 metres heigth is carried in grand procession between two of the main churches of the town.

Cesarò: In the Mt. Soro range of the southern Nebrodi Mountains this village stands on the watershed between the Cuto and Troina streams. In 1334 Frederick II of Aragon donated the village to Cristoforo Romano Colonna, an important doctor from Messina.

The economy is based on same small cottage industries and on agriculture.

Little of the castle has survived. The main church is baroque, houses a 15th century Crucifix painted on a tablet. This is the place of lovers of mountain-excursions. Nearby is the Femmina Morta pass. Near Cesarò you get splendid views embracing the western slopes of Etna, woods and an artificial lake, the so-called Biviere di Cesarò. The many possible excursions are best made with the aid of a guide.

Fiumedinisi: In the south eastern Peloritan mountains, the village is clustered in a bend of the Fiumedinisi river, close to its mouth.

It is surrounded by beautiful mountains and small, rich valleys protected by a nature reserve. The most important monument is the castle "Belvedere" which is a medieval fortress at 750 metres a.s.l. with a breathtaking view on the Mediterranean Sea. It is a place that oozes a rare charm for the loneliness of the ruins and the majesty of the landscape(dr Andrea Orlando).

The main church conserves two 16th C. sculptures, by the Florentine M. Montanini and the artist from Messina R. Bonanno.

Floresta: Floresta (also *Casal Floresta*) is the highest Sicilian village, lying 1,275 meters above sea level in the Nebrodi Nature Park in a saddle between Mt Pistone and the Serre di Baratta. Its foundation seems to date back to when the Romans invaded and colonized Sicily; a time when the area was originally dense forest (floresta in

Latin), with tall trees used by the Romans for building their ships and boats. Today the immense florest are gone but it is still one of the coldest village of south Italy having regularly about two metres snow each year.

Forza D'agrò: It is basically a medieval village dramatically overlooking the Ionian Sea at 15 Km (9 miles) from Taormina. Impressing are the surrounding spurs of the southern Peloritani mountains carved by the rivers which in winter erode their rocky banks.

The winding route to the village opens sweeping views of the coasts of Taormina and Calabria as far as the Strait of Messina. The village is dominated by the remains of the castle of the 16th century, today used as a cemetery. Forza d'Agrò has featured as the backdrop in a number of films, such as *The Godfather* trilogy.

Francavilla: Francavilla di Sicilia is a medieval city which grew around a norman castle and the basilian monastery of San Salvatore di Placa, founded in 1092 upon the ruins of another. We suggest to visit the old church Matrice (1493), whose main door is decorated with a vine leaf motif, and the convent of the Cappucini (1585) and its museum. The Cappucini convent, built in 1585, is still in good condition. There is a splendid carved wood altar and two precious painted wood relics in the church. The name "Francavilla" comes from the French *franc-ville*, that is "Free town" because originally it was a tax-free town.

Gallodoro: Situated in the southern Peloritans mountains to the left of the Letojanni river, this village is not far from the Ionian coast. Formerly part of the Taormina territory, in 1952 it became independent.

Giardini Naxos: Situated below Taormina, with his lovely bay, a splendid sea, in a flat coastal position. Naxos was the first Greek colony in Sicily, founded in 735 B.C. by Chalcidians of Euboea. To commemorate the event, a monument in bronze was erected at the very tip of Naxos Capo Schisó: the *NIKE.*

Naxos is archeologically one of the very few remaining chances to study the most ancient aspects of Greek urbanistics.The fertile sunny position, convenient for boats, must have been the reason for the choice made by the colonizers.From the 18th C. onwards the village of citrus farmers and fishermen lived simply in this "village of gardens", that's where the name Giardini (Gardens) comes from. A visitor to Giardini will also recall that Garibaldi (the italian hero who unified Italy starting a liberation-expedition from

Sicily) left from the port of Giardini to land in Calabria. A monument commemorates the event.

Gorges Of Alcantara: The river Alcantara marks the boundary between the Provinces of Messina and Catania. The Greeks called the river "Akesines", the Arabs "Al-Quàntarah" ("the bridge"). Along 48 Km (30 miles) of its lenght it brushes up against the territory of Randazzo and flows on towards the coast, separating the volcano Mt. Etna from the mountains to the north.

The spectacular gorges were created by the erosion and cooling of the lava flowing from the crater of Mount Dolce, between Linguaglossa and Randazzo, on the Etna massif.

The gorges show the inner part of the flow with the splendid, columnar fissures of magma rapidly cooled by the gushing water. More than 20m (57 ft) deep the gorges have bizzarre basalt prisms dotted here and there with cool spontaneous vegetation.

Itàla: Situated in the south eastern Peloritan mountains, Itála lies on the southern slopes of Monte Scuderi. The houses are scattered on the banks of the Itála river. Marina d'Itála is situated at its outlet to the Ionian sea. Existing in Norman times, the village was donated by Roger to the monastery of San Pietro, built by him. From 1928 to 1947 the village was annexed to that of Scaletta Zanclea. Its economy is based on agriculture, commerce, summer tourism and wood working.

The main church conserves two precious 14th century painted crucifixes. In the Croce district the Church of San Pietro (1093) has conserved the traits of the Norman Basilian construction: it has a Basilica plan with three naves and three apses, the exterior enlivened with blind and tiered arches in fired brick and limestone.

Letojanni: Situated on the Ionian coast north of Taormina, Letojanni extends along the eastern Sicilian trunk road, on both sides of the outlet of the Letojanni river. A small hamlet coming under Gallodoro, it expanded in the last century and with Gallodoro in 1880 it obtained administrational equality, maintained until 1952 when Letojanni and Gallodoro became two autonomous communes.

Tourism has developed here, favored by good reception facilities, and flanks agriculture and fishing.

Mandanici: This village is in the Peloritan mountains at the southern foot of Mount Cavallo. Mandanichium belonged to the Basilian monastery, founded by Roger the Norman, until 1475, when it passed to the secular clergy.

The land is filled with vineyards, olive groves, orchards, woods and pasturelands, favoring stock rearing.

<u>Savoca:</u> Savoca is situated on the low southern slopes of the Peloritan mountains. It was founded in the first half of the 12th century and was first mentioned in 1415 when it already belonged to the archibishops of Messina. The economy is agricultural and based mainly on the cultivation of citrus fruits.

Only ruins remain those of the norman castle. The church of San Michele, 15th century in origin, has two lovely gothic doors and houses a coeval painting of San Michele. The main Church, erected in the 16th century, has a lovely Renaissance door, two smaller gothic doors and a rose window;

alongside it is a 15th C. bell tower. The town, together with Forza d'Agrò, was the location for the scenes set in Corleone of Francis Ford Coppola's *The Godfather*. The place is also famous for the Capuchin monastery where mummified bodies of prestigious town residents of 18th and 19th centuries are on display.

Top Things to Do in Taormina

Taormina is often characterized as overly touristy and during the peak season it can get crowded, especially when the cruise ships are in port. While many folks may feel that Taormina can be done quickly in one day, I think a couple of days is more appropriate to cover not only Taormina, but some of the surrounding sites as well. Undoubtedly, Taormina is one of the most picturesque locations in all of Italy and can rival the Amalfi Coast and Cinque Terre for sheer natural beauty. If you're planning on a couple of days in Taormina, this guide will help you to cover all of the must see sites and a few more for the more adventurous souls.

Greco Teatro

Taormina's Greco Roman Theater is probably the most visited and photographed site is all of Sicily and for good reason. The site is simply spectacular. Perched on a hill overlooking the Ionian Sea, and with a perfect view of Mount Etna looming in the distance, it makes for an absolutely beautiful setting. The ancient theatre is built mostly of brick, which would indicate that it is of Roman origins, but its layout follows what is considered to be a Greek design so it is sometimes referred to as the Greco Roman Theatre. Most likely the theatre was of Greek origins and then rebuilt on its present site by the Romans. No matter its origin, the theatre is a must see on any visit to Taormina.

Because of its remarkable preservation the theatre is still used today for concerts and theatre performances. If you happen to be in Taormina during a performance look into attending a show here for an unforgettable experience.

Castelmola

Located on the top of a hill above Taormina is the quaint village of Castelmola. Considered one of the most beautiful towns in all of Italy its precarious setting high above Taormina provides for an amazing view of Taormina, the beaches of Giardini Naxos, and Mount Etna.

The Duomo of Castelmola, also known as the church of San Niccolo' di Bari, is worth a visit and has a balcony which affords some great views. The remains of the castle itself are not much, but it is worth the few extra steps to climb to the ruins of the castle if for no other reason than the view. The village is a great spot for a mid day lunch break and some shopping.

Getting to Castelmola can be done with a short taxi ride or you can take the bus. The bus station is a ten minute walk from the center of Taormina and the bus trip takes about fifteen minutes. For the adventurous souls out there you can walk/hike up to Castelmola. Plan on at least an hour each way and possibly more depending on your physical condition.

Alcantara Gorge

The Alcantara Gorge is something that I highly recommend. As it's about a 40 minute bus ride from Taormina you should probably dedicate at least half a day for a visit here. Located on the north side of Mount Etna, the Gorge was formed thousands of years ago when a lava flow from the volcano was cooled quickly by the flow of the

Alcantara River. This quick cooling resulted in the lava forming columns through which the river eroded a channel, eventually resulting in the gorge that you see today.

There is a beautiful path that you can walk that follows the top of the gorge and you get some great views looking down into the gorge from this vantage point. You can also take an elevator down to the river where there is a small beach where you can swim, sunbathe, and walk the shallow river if you like. For the more adventurous, you can do some river trekking with a guide and the appropriate equipment can be rented here if you like.

A visit to the Alcantara Gorge is a great break from the crowds of Taormina. The site has facilities including a restaurant and the bus stop is right at the front gate to the Gorge site.

Tip

Be sure to bring your bathing suit, water shoes and a towel. The water is advertised as being very cold but we found it refreshing.

Public Gardens

Many visitors either bypass the public gardens or are simply not aware that they are here. I found the gardens to be a beautiful shady respite from the crowded Corso Umberto. Also known as the Trevelyan Gardens, this English-style garden has a panoramic walkway that faces the sea and Mount Etna. Numerous flower beds, bushes, trees and finely trimmed hedges adorn the garden and make for a pleasant walk or a great spot to just sit and admire the view.

The garden also contains a few old artillery pieces from WWII, a play area for children and a few cottages and towers. A small terrace area is also found here and is used for small outdoor concerts or gatherings. If you're looking for a break from the hustle and bustle of Taormina head to the public gardens for a little rest and relaxation.

Piazza Duomo

This beautiful piazza is located at the western end of the Corso Umberto in the old section of Taormina, and is the site of the Church of San Nicola, otherwise known as the Duomo of Taormina. The church was built around 1400 AD and was constructed over the site of an older church.

At the center of the piazza is a Baroque fountain that contains a centaur (from Greek mythology part human, part horse), which is the symbol of Taormina. This small but beautiful piazza is the perfect place to relax and unwind for a spell.

Tip

Be sure to take a drink from one of the horse fountains. Do you see them in the photo below?

Shop & Stroll the Corso Umberto

The Corso Umberto is the main pedestrian street through Taormina and is hard to miss. For the shoppers out there this is the place to be. The Corso Umberto is lined with numerous high end shops as well as gelato shops, produce vendors, café's, souvenir and jewelry shops. No matter what you are looking for it's a sure bet that you can find it somewhere along the Corso Umberto. At night the street comes alive with music and entertainment and can resemble a party atmosphere. It all makes for a fun and lively place to be.

Mount Etna

When visiting Taormina, Mount Etna looks so close you'd think you could reach out and touch it. One of the things that helps make Taormina such a beautiful and picturesque place is the fact that you can get a great view of Mount Etna from pretty much anywhere in Taormina. Taking pictures and looking at Mount Etna is wonderful, but making a visit to Europe's largest Volcano is an amazing adventure.

There are numerous tours available from Taormina that will pick you up and take to you the Sapienza Refuge area, which is 1910 meters up the mountain. This is the only one of the five refuge areas that is accessible by public transportation. Because of this it is the most popular of the five hubs for accessing Mount Etna. The refuge areas all have basic overnight accommodations and restaurants if you're looking to spend a night on the mountain.

From the Sapienza area you have a few options available to you. There are numerous trails from here where you can hike and explore the area. Or, you can take the cable car farther up the mountain to some of the more recent eruption sites. If you want to go still higher there are four-wheel drive buses that will take you as high as is permissible given the status of the mountain. Keep in mind that Mount Etna is not only Europe's largest volcano but it is also it's most active. Another consideration to keep in mind when planning a visit to Mount Etna is the cost. The cable car and four-wheel drive buses are very expensive so make sure you are prepared for the cost as well as the elements when making your visit. Even at the Sapienza Refuge area the weather can be extremely cold and windy so come prepared.

Tip

Be sure to bring warm clothing and sturdy shoes. The footing is loose, broken lava, so watch your step especially going downhill.

BamBar

To be honest it wasn't until just before we were to leave for Italy that I came across the BamBar. Apparently this place is somewhat of a local legend in Taormina. Famous for their Granita, which is a semi-frozen dessert that originated in Sicily, the establishment has been visited by numerous high-profile celebrities over the years. The owner, who may very well also be your server, will be glad to show you the long list of celebrities who have graced his little bar. It was clear to us that he is not only proud of his famous cliental but also of his world famous Granita.

Located off of the main street in a small piazza with outdoor seating, it's a great place to relax for a few minutes while enjoying one of Taormina's famous desserts. The BamBar's Granita is consistently ranked among the best in all of Sicily. It comes in numerous flavors and can be served with or without cream. I had the peach and it was wonderful.

Piazza IX Aprile

It would seem that Piazza IX Aprile (Square of the 9th April) is the epicenter of Taormina. This beautiful piazza with is black and white pavers seems to draw everyone in Taormina at sunset for a great photo opportunity. From here you have an unobstructed view of Mount Etna and the Ionian Sea. Standing guard to the piazza are two churches, St. Augustine's and the Church of St. Joseph. At the western end of the piazza is the Porta Di Mezzo, which takes visitors under the Clock Tower and into the oldest part of Taormina.

The Piazza IX Aprile makes for a great meeting place and with its many benches is a perfect spot to sit and people watch or simply stare off into the stunning view. You may even be lucky enough to catch a wedding ceremony coming out of the Church. At night the square comes alive as musicians and artists fill the piazza with music and color.

If you find yourself planning a visit to Taormina, I hope you found this guide helpful. My opinion of Taormina is that it is certainly worth more than a day to fully enjoy all that the area has to offer. It is also possibly the most beautiful place that you will visit in Sicily. Enjoy your stay.

Where to stay in Taormina

It's a good idea to learn a bit about Taormina's geography before you book accommodation, as hotels, B&BS and holiday apartments are scattered over a variety of locations in the area, and these will offer very different holiday experiences. Where to stay in Taormina really depends on what kind of holiday you're planning, and your budget. There are hotels, B&Bs and holiday apartments in the historic centre, in picturesque spots further afield, and in locations by the sea nearby. On this page you'll find a guide to the accommodation options and a selection of the best places to stay.

Taormina is one of Italy's smartest tourist destinations, and there are several very grand and long-established hotels in the town, as well as smart and expensive modern hotels offering a luxury experience. There are also cheaper options including simpler hotels and B&Bs. As this is a very popular resort, though, the prices are generally higher than you'll find elsewhere in Sicily, so it pays to plan and book well in advance to find the best affordable options.

Tips

Taormina is a fairly expensive place to stay, but shopping around in advance can find you some affordable accommodation options - especially if you avoid the peak summer season. Staying in spring or autumn means you could enjoy good weather without the crowds and at cheaper prices. If you're staying on a budget, note that cheaper accommodation may not offer much in the way of breakfast, or of pleasant areas for relaxing, though the town itself has plenty of bars and public spaces to compensate. Restaurants are uncommon in Italian hotels, so proximity to the town centre makes evening dining easier. B&Bs and apartments can offer good-value independent accommodation, but do make sure these establishments have plenty of positive reviews, and read the small print regarding arrival times, left luggage availability and any extra charges. If you have a car, check whether hotels offer parking and if there is an extra charge for this.

Where to stay

The historic centre

The historic centre (*centro storico*) of Taormina is located on a saddle in the hills high above the sea. The old town was once walled and fairly narrow, with a town gateway (still standing) at each end of the long main street. This picturesque street, Corso Umberto, is still the most important and lively thoroughfare. Largely pedestrianised, it's picturesque and lined with shops, cafés, restaurants and galleries. Staying in the historic centre is the best way to enjoy the elegant and lively resort atmosphere of Taormina. Once the daytrippers have gone, the lanes become much less crowded, with a more 'exclusive' feel, as residents and those spending the night in Taormina mingle in an evening *passeggiata*.

This is my favourite area to stay in Taormina, to get the full experience of the town. The drawbacks are that it's less convenient for driving and for public transport (you'll have to walk out of the town gates to pick up buses and taxis), the old buildings and narrow lanes mean you won't always get balconies and big views and you might hear noise from restaurants and bars. There aren't many hotels right in the heart of the historic centre; there are more B&Bs and apartments. Although this is generally the most expensive area to stay in, there are cheaper options. A selection including a good budget hotel is listed further down this page.

Outside the centre

Modern Taormina sprawls along any available bit of slope that's not too steep either side of the historic centre. Roads wind off through residential areas, and you'll find larger, more modern hotels in these areas as well as B&Bs. Many are still in comfortable walking distance of the historic centre, so if you're getting better facilities and cheaper prices, they will make a good compromise as an accommodation choice. Others are further afield, and it's a good idea to both look at the location map provided in hotel listings, and read the comments of previous guests to get an idea of how convenient the position really is. Some roads are busy and routes may be steep, which will make a difference to walkability. A location at the north-eastern end of town (outside the Porta Messina town gate) will be more convenient for public transport and for taking the cable-car down to the beach.

By the seaside

Although Taormina has excellent views over the Ionian Sea, it is located high above sea level. Staying down by the sea will give you a very different type of vacation: a beach holiday with the opportunity to pay visits to Taormina taking the bus, cable-car or taxi. There are walking routes between Giardini Naxos (the station area) and Taormina and Mazzarò and Taormina, but only suitable for energetic walkers (and at my last visit the Giardini footpath was blocked by landslides).

The beach resort of Giardini Naxos is an established seaside town with its own character, a long narrow beach, cheaper places to stay and buses up to Taormina. You won't find the best beaches in Sicily along this coastline, but there are small stretches of sand and pebbles, with beach establishments hiring out sunbeds and parasols as well as 'free beach' areas. The sandiest areas are at Giardini Naxos and Recanati, to its south, and north of Taormina along the coast around Letojanni.

More directly below Taormina, there are headlands and a couple of small bays, with hotels and other buildings grouped around them. The Isola Bella cove is pretty with its little island and beach, and a short walk to the north is Mazzarò, a settlement around another bay. Staying along this stretch of shore will give you easy sea access, the possibility of picturesque sea views and proximity to the coast road. Although these bays aren't big and are pebbly, they have the best access to Taormina via a cable-car from Mazzarò, and by bus.

The best places to stay in Taormina by selection

Hotels

Belmond Grand Hotel Timeo

Taormina's Belmond Grand Hotel Timeo is opposite the Greek Theatre and offers panoramic views of Mount Etna and the Sicilian Coast. It features an outdoor pool and spa.

Rooms at Belmond Grand Hotel Timeo are all air conditioned and offer, satellite TV, minibar, private bathroom and free Wi-Fi. Some rooms have views of the sea or the hotel gardens with magnolias, cypress and palm trees.

Belmond Grand Hotel Timeo serves an American buffet breakfast. The restaurant serves both Sicilian and Mediterranean cooking, and Literary Terrace & Bar provides drinks and snacks on its sea-view terrace.

The wellness centre at Belmond Grand Hotel Timeo includes a sauna, Turkish bath, gym and massage services. Guests can also relax on the nearby private beach, using the free beach shuttle service.

Belmond Grand Hotel Timeo is 5 km from the Taormina-Giardini Naxos Train Station and 45 minutes' drive from Catania Airport. Private transfers can be arranged to and from the airport and train station.

This property also has one of the best-rated locations in Taormina! Guests are happier about it compared to other properties in the area.

Hotel Taodomus

Taodomus is a boutique hotel set on Corso Umberto I in the heart of Taormina. It features a panoramic terrace overlooking Mount Etna and the bay and offers free Wi-Fi.

This cosy hotel has just 10 guest rooms, all with air conditioning. A free internet point is available in the business centre, together with free Wi-Fi internet access in the entire hotel.

Breakfast is served on the terrace or in the comfort of your room at no extra cost. It features local products and organic ingredients.

Hotel Taodomus is set in the heart of the historic centre, a 10-minute walk from the Greek Amphitheatre.

Subject to availability, guests can use the swimming pool at a nearby hotel at an extra charge.

This property also has one of the best-rated locations in Taormina! Guests are happier about it compared to other properties in the area.

Couples particularly like the location they rated it 9.8 for a two-person trip.

This property is also rated for the best value in Taormina! Guests are getting more for their money when compared to other properties in this city.

Hotel Victoria

Offering attentive personal service, Hotel Victoria is located on Taormina's Corso Umberto I, just 300 m from the Greek Theatre. It has traditionally furnished rooms with air conditioning and satellite TV.

Rooms at the family-run Victoria are fitted with wrought-iron beds and natural wood furniture. Each comes with a private bathroom with shower and hairdryer.

An Italian buffet breakfast is provided in the Baroque-style dining room. Guests can enjoy cappuccino or herbal tea with freshly made pastries.

Staff at the Victoria Hotel are available 24 hours a day, and can advise on trips to the Palazzo Duca di Santo Stefano or the Palazzo Corvaja, both a 5-minute walk away.

This property also has one of the best-rated locations in Taormina! Guests are happier about it compared to other properties in the area.

Couples particularly like the location they rated it 9.8 for a two-person trip.

This property is also rated for the best value in Taormina! Guests are getting more for their money when compared to other properties in this city

Casa Cuseni Maison De Charme
Just a 5-minute walk from Taormina's main square, Casa Cuseni Maison De Charme is a historical B&B housed in a museum of fine arts declared a

national monument. The building and its historic garden were designed by Frank Brangwyn, and are complete with 13 panoramic terraces, 7 fountains, and rare plants.

Each room at Casa Cuseni Maison De Charme has a balcony with views of the Naxos Gulf and Mount Etna. They all come with air conditioning and Sicilian furniture of the 17th and 18th centuries.

Set in a listed villa, the interiors are decorated with works by Picasso, Henry Faulkner, and other masters of the 20th century. The list of famous guests includes philosopher Bertrand Russell, novelist Roald Dahl, and actress Greta Garbo.

Sweet and savoury food can be enjoyed at breakfast, with gluten-free items available on request. This daily treat can be served in the breakfast room with views over Mount Etna or the

Mediterranean Sea, or on the terrace when the weather is good.

This property also has one of the best-rated locations in Taormina! Guests are happier about it compared to other properties in the area.

Couples particularly like the location they rated it **9.8** for a two-person trip.

This property is also rated for the best value in Taormina! Guests are getting more for their money when compared to other properties in this city.

TaoApartments - Casa Vittoria

Located 1.2 km from Isola Bella in Taormina, this apartment features a terrace. The apartment is 1.2 km from Mazzaro. Free WiFi is featured throughout the property.

There is a seating area, a dining area and a kitchen. Towels and bed linen are offered in this self-catering accommodation. Other facilities at Casa Vittoria include a sun terrace.

Corso Umberto is 400 m from Casa Vittoria, while Taormina Cathedral is 500 m from the property. The nearest airport is Catania Fontanarossa Airport, 65 km from the property.

This property also has one of the best-rated locations in Taormina! Guests are happier about it compared to other properties in the area.

Couples particularly like the location they rated it **10** for a two-person trip.

This property is also rated for the best value in Taormina! Guests are getting more for their money when compared to other properties in this city.

Villa Astoria

Family-run Villa Astoria has a garden and panoramic sea views just 500 m from Taormina's historic centre. The hotel is 2 minutes' walk from the cableway to Mazzarò and Isola Bella beaches.

Each room is decorated with antique furniture, some have a sea-view balcony. Modern amenities include air conditioning and satellite TV with international channels.

Buses stop right outside and connect you to Catania Airport, and other places of interest around Sicily. Private parking is possible upon reservation.

Couples particularly like the location they rated it 9.5 for a two-person trip.

This property is also rated for the best value in Taormina! Guests are getting more for their money when compared to other properties in this city.

Hotel Villa Belvedere

The Belvedere is an elegant villa with views of Naxos Bay and Mount Etna in the distance. It is next to public gardens, and a 5 minutes' walk from Taormina's Corso Umberto.

Hotel Villa Belvedere offers classic rooms with elegant furniture and air conditioning. Most rooms overlook the sea, the gardens or the summer outdoor swimming pool. Free Wi-Fi is available throughout.

The villa is surrounded by terraced gardens filled with flowers and palm trees. The panoramic swimming pool is set on a sun terrace with sun beds and parasols.

The restaurant is also located by the pool. It serves traditional Sicilian cuisine for lunch.

When booking a room with a breakfast-included option, a generous buffet is served between 07:30 and 11:00 in a sun-lit breakfast room with sea and garden views. Early breakfast is available on request.

Couples particularly like the location they rated it 9.6 for a two-person trip.

This property is also rated for the best value in Taormina! Guests are getting more for their money when compared to other properties in this city.

Hotel Villa Ducale
Villa Ducale is a small, luxurious boutique hotel with outstanding views of the sea, Mount Etna and the Strait of Messina. It features free WiFi in public

areas, an outdoor hot tub, and a sun terrace with loungers.

The strategic location of Hotel Villa Ducale combines the tranquillity of a panoramic spot and the proximity to the town centre, a 25-minute walk away. The hotel offers a free shuttle service to the centre of Taormina, and an airport shuttle is available on request.

Villa Ducale is renowned for its rich breakfast buffet with homemade Sicilian specialities, served on the panoramic terrace. Restaurant service is available throughout the day, and the hotel features a popular cocktail buffet every evening.

Couples particularly like the location they rated it 9.3 for a two-person trip.

This property is also rated for the best value in Taormina! Guests are getting more for their money when compared to other properties in this city

Casa Lucia
Set within 11 km of Isola Bella and 11 km of Mazzaro in Taormina, Casa Lucia offers accommodation with free WiFi and seating area.

All units here are air-conditioned and feature a flat-screen TV, a living room with a sofa, a well-equipped kitchen with a dining area, and a private bathroom with bidet, a hair dryer and free toiletries. A fridge and oven are also offered, as well as a kettle.

A terrace is available for guests to use at the apartment.

Taormina Cathedral is 6 km from Casa Lucia, while Corso Umberto is 6 km from the property. The nearest airport is Catania Fontanarossa Airport, 64 km from the accommodation.

Couples particularly like the location they rated it 8.9 for a two-person trip.

This property is also rated for the best value in Taormina! Guests are getting more for their money when compared to other properties in this city.

UNAHOTELS Capotaormina

UNAHOTELS Capotaormina is perched on a rock below Taormina and is surrounded by the sea, offering an amazing view of the fantastic Giardini Naxos Bay and Isola Bella Island.

This pleasant building is set against the unusual background of Mount Etna with its snowy peaks, and all the hotel rooms are equipped with a balcony. Classic rooms offer garden views, superior rooms offer a full sea view.

Staying at the Capotaormina you can enjoy spending pleasant hours on the private beach, accessible through a lift carved into the rock. The beach and the hotel's sea-water swimming pool are equipped with sun beds, parasols and beach towels, for your relaxation and enjoyment.

The regenerating experience continues in the 14-person hot tub with purified sea water, in the gym with trainer and beauty salon.

The property also provides daily newspapers, a jeweller's, a garage, and an outdoor car park with limited places. A free shuttle bus to/from Taormina centre is also available, and boat excursions can be booked during summer.

The hotel's 3 restaurants serve international, Sicilian and Mediterranean cuisine.

Couples particularly like the location they rated it 9.5 for a two-person trip.

Panoramic Hotel

Located 20 m from the beach on Isola Bella Bay, Panoramic Hotel is linked to Taormina's historic centre by cable car. All rooms and the outdoor swimming pool have Mediterranean Sea views.

This modern 4-star hotel overlooks the Isola Bella WWF Nature Reserve and its namesake island. A few steps take you directly down to the beach.

With contemporary interior design and hand-crafted furniture, rooms here are elegant and unique. Each one has its own balcony and includes air conditioning, free Wi-Fi and an LCD TV. Bathrooms are decorated in mosaics and include a hairdryer.

Breakfast at Hotel Panoramic is buffet style and is served out on the rooftop terrace. Here you will also find the pool and poolside bar serving cocktails.

Multilingual staff can organise airport transfers and excursions around the island of Sicily. Reception is open 24-hours a day and has a luggage porter.

Villa Arianna B&B
Situated in a raised position overlooking the beautiful Mazzarò Bay and Taormina Beach the family-run Villa Arianna is 700 m from Isola Bella island. It offers free Wi-Fi and elegant rooms.

Spacious and air conditioned, rooms come with a 42" Plasma TV, an extra large double bed and LED lighting. Each has a private bathroom with soft bathrobes while most boast a large equipped terrace with panoramic sea views.

A sweet Italian-style breakfast is available daily on request, and can be served on the sunny terrace or in the comfort of your room. The Arianna has a small shop where guests can sample and buy Sicilian and national wines.

A cable car is located near the property and links to the centre of Taormina in 3 minutes. Catania and Messina can be reached within 30 minutes' drive, while Mount Etna is 33 km away.

This property also has one of the best-rated locations in Taormina! Guests are happier about it compared to other properties in the area.

Getting there

Taormina is Sicily's main tourist destination; it is well serviced by important roads as well as by train and is also conveniently reachable by plane.

By car: From Palermo take highway A19 Palermo-Catania and continue on A18 until destination. From Siracusa take the state road 114 to Catania and then take highway A18 until the exit at Taormina. From Agrigento take state highway 640 for Caltanisetta, continue then on highway A19 to Catania and then get on the A18 until destination. From Trapanitake A29 towards Palermo, continue on A19 Palermo-Catania and then take A18 up to destination.

Those coming from Continental Italy must continue on highway A3 Salerno-Reggio Calabria and exit on Villa San Giovanni to board the ferries that go to Messina. From Messina, highway A18 will get you in no time to Taormina.

By train: Taormina is on the Messina-Catania line with direct and very frequent trains going both ways. If you are coming from Palermo or from other cities in Sicily, you will have to change trains. From Rome there are some direct trains for Taormina (via Naples), the trip lasts 9-10 hours. For times please consult the Trenitalia site or call the green number 89 20 21.

By plane: The International Airport of Catania (CTA) is 50 km from Taormina. The airport offers connections with all the major Italian and European cities, including all the capitals. From the airport the Alibus shuttle service goes to Catania station every 20 minutes. There is a direct bus available from Etna Trasporti linking the Airport with Taormina.

Events

Taormina Events, Italy

All the artistic and cultural events in Taormina take place in the summer, when the city is at its best and there are crowds of tourists. For this reason, if you a planning a trip to this area between June and September, we strongly advise you to book your hotel in Taormina well in advance.

Taormina Arte June/July/August

It is one of the most famous events in Sicily. A Festival dedicated to music, from symphonies to rock, dance and theater during which famous artists from all over the world come to perform in the wonderful, beautiful setting of the Ancient Theater. One section of the Festival over the years has become so popular that it has become an event in itself: the Taormina Film Festival.

Taormina Film Festival June

After the International Film Festival in Venice, this is the oldest film festival in Italy. World-famous guests, film directors, script-writers, composers from Hollywood and independent ones too all come to the festival, whether they are busy or not. The setting is the amazing Ancient Theater of

Taormina. At the end of the Festival, that usually lasts a week, there is the awards ceremony, during which the Nastri d'Argento for Italian cinema are handed out, a prestigious award that is much sought after by our national artists. In addition to the competitions, there are also retrospective sessions and side-sections with a specific theme.

Madonna della Rocca September
The statue of the Madonna della Rocca is housed in a sanctuary between Taormina and Castelmola. In the second weekend of September, a religious procession carries the statue from the sanctuary to the town where a large banquet is organized, to eat "carne infornata": lamb cooked with spices and herbs in a wood-fire oven.

Other festivals and fairs that are regular events in Taormina are the Sagra del Costume e del Carretto Siciliani Traditional Costume and Sicilian Cart Fair (May), the Festa Patronale di San Pancrazio San

Pancrazio Patron Saint Festival (once every four years in July) and Carnival (February)

The End

Printed in Great Britain
by Amazon